INDEX

KASHMIR VALLEY - A TOURIST PARADISE

"Gar Firdaus bar rue zamin ast

Hamin ast, Hamin ast, Hamin ast"

(If there is a Paradise on Earth

It is this, It is this, It is this)

(Emperor Jahangir)

"Terrorism and tourism rhyme with each other. Yet they don't go well alongside despite some similarities shared. If one booms it is doomsday to the other. It is sheer juxtaposition between the two lucrative industries in the city of the lights left in a city of plight."

Indeewara Jayawardane

Kashmir is a stunning and captivating land that abounds with natural beauty. Adorned by snow-capped mountains, wildflower meadows, immense glaciers, and sparkling lakes, Kashmir has often been likened to heaven on earth. Valley is Globe's most distinctive landmark. The magical beauty of lovely lake-dotted Valley, located at five thousand feet above sea, carpeted by snow, is no doubt a "Paradise on Earth" The Great Himalayas and the Pir Panjal, surround the Valley from north and south respectively, different mountain passes provide only entrance and exist to this Valley. Thus mighty Himalayan ranges provide a natural protection from invaders. Despite such natural barriers and isolation, invaders are often attracted towards this Valley for rich wealth, mysterious beauty, true knowledge, exquisite artisanship and cultural heritage. Land of such strategic location with rare amalgamation of positive aspects, scenic beauty and splendid seasons must be flocked by tourists from all over the world year around. No doubt, tourists flocked this land of unending glory since time immemorial. Unfortunately outbreak of terror incidents from 1989 toppled tourist inflow towards Valley.

Jammu and Kashmir, the land of unique and chequered history abounds in ancient literature, language, religion, arts and crafts, music and dance. It is like a jewel in the map of India. Located at the northernmost part of India, the region spreads between 32^0 17' to 36^0 58' North latitude and 73^0 26' to 80^0 30' East longitude occupying a total area of 2, 22,236 Sq Kms including 78,114 sq km under illegal occupation of Pakistan, 5,180 Sq kms handed over by Pakistan to China, and 37,555 Sq kms is under illegal occupation of china. (Dhar, 2008a). Bounded on the south by Himachal Pradesh and the Punjab on the south west, Pakistan on the west, on the north by Chinese Turkistan and a little of Russian Turkistan, and on the east by Chinese Tibet, Jammu and Kashmir shares international boundaries with Pakistan, China and Tibet. Occupying such a strategic location, this spectacular landscape is filled with snow covered mountain peaks, lakes, honey-dewed orchards, lush green and flower carpeted meadows, thick forest, blue skies which beckon every one about its legendary beauty and unending charm from times immemorial till date. The numerous civilizations that have inhabited *the region from time to time have left their impressions on the culture of Jammu and Kashmir. As a result, apart from its renowned physical beauty, it is also well known for its diverse and rich natural and cultural heritage. The Jammu and Kashmir state accounts for 3.2% of total geographical area of India making it the 11th largest state of the country. Forest area of the state is 20,230 Sq. Km. which constitutes 19.95% of its geographical area. Varied and diversified geographical location, hills, and inhospitable terrain, vulnerability to natural disasters, agro-climatic and topographic features, remoteness and poor connectivity, isolation from major markets, scattered population, and lack of economic infrastructure, weak resource base, sparse population density, shallow markets presents very peculiar and unique problems to the State of Jammu and Kashmir. The State is connected to the rest of the country through highway NH 1A, 400 Kms stretch (approx) maintained by Border Roads Organization (BRO) of India. The Jammu-Srinagar National Highway (NH1A), the lifeline of Kashmir Valley is considered to be the most expensive road for maintenance. The state of Jammu and Kashmir in contrast to other states has got two capitals cities, Srinagar (Summer Capital of J&K State) and Jammu (Winter Capital of J&K State). Based on the distinct geographical and social features, the state is divided into three regions - Jammu, the Kashmir Valley and Ladakh. Jammu occupies the region between the outer hills region bounding the valley of Kashmir in the south and the plains of Punjab. Rugged hills varying in heights from 600 mts to 1,200 mts above the sea level run parallel to one another and give way in the north and northeast to the outer hills of the Shiwaliks, varying in height form 1,200 mts to 3,600 mts above the sea level. These are comfortably named as 'middle hills' or the 'Middle Himalayas', occupying 26,263 Sq. Km. in area. This is the second largest division in the state. River Ravi flows in the east of this region and the river Jhelum in the west. Chenab flows through the Jammu district before entering Pakistan. Relatively warm climate lasts from April to June followed by rainy season from July to September and winter season from October to March. Coniferous forest thickly covers the upper reaches and silver fir, deodar, spruce, oak and pine trees cover the lower regions of 'Outer Hill' and 'Middle Mountain'. Cactus varieties of bushes and trees occupy the 'plains area'. Maize, rice, millet, barley and wheat are the main crops of the region. Jammu region is well known for its rich mineral deposits. Coal, bauxite, copper, Zinc and lead are abundant in this region. Panthers, black and red bear, wild goat, ibex, musk deer, wolf, fox, pig, leopard are found in the forests of Jammu region. Area 26,293 Sq. km. Important Tourist Attractions of Jammu Division are Katra, Patnitop, Sanasar, Batote, Mantalai, Mansar Lake, Akhnoor, Dogra Art Gallery, Raghunath Temple, Peer Khoh, Peer Baba, Ziarat Baba Buddan Shah Idgah, Ziarat Baba Roshan Shah Wali Idgah, Ziarat Peer Mitha Idgah, Shri Guru Nanak Dev Ji Gurudwara, Talli Sahib Gurudwara, Nangali Sahib Gurudwara Protestant church on Wazarat road, Roman Catholic Church near Jewel Chowk, Shri Mata Vaishno Devi Shrine, Shahdara Sharief, Buddha Amarnath, Bahu Fort / Temple, Shri Shiv Khori, Resai Fort, Manasar Lake, Patnitop, Krimchi, Ramnagar Fort, Barbore Temples, Poonch Fort, Ramkund, Basholi, Shahdara Sharif, Samot Sar and Chingus are some of the famous tourist spots and pilgrimage centre which attract lot of tourist towards it every year. The greatest advantage of all these destinations in Jammu division is that it is opened to tourist year around and is well connected by road and rail networks. Ladakh "... the Moonland... the most remote region of India" (Sajnani, 2001), Beyond the valley of Kashmir, mountainous terrain extending to the Chinese border on the north, merging into Tibet in the east and is surrounded along the south by the extension of Great Himalayan range forms the Ladakh region where the mighty mountain peak seems to touch the sky. Accommodating the world's second highest peak K2 and the famous Karakoram pass (5,517.64m) which facilitate direct route from India to China, and spreading over 96,701 Sq. Km. Ladakh division is the biggest of Jammu and Kashmir. Housing High Mountains with average height between 5000 and 7000m, head waters of rivers like the Indus, the Sutlej and the Chenab though found in this region, ironically the land is devoid of any vegetation. Despite such constraints, this unique region offers enchanting landscape, breathtaking scenic beauty, variegated moods of nature, glaciers and snow capped mountains surrounding the crystal-clear lakes. The Ladakh provides matchless picturesque sights to viewers than in any part of the world. It looks almost like an empty land filled with wonders. World's highest road, the road to Khardung La – 5600 mts above sea level, the pangong salt water lake stretching about 112 kms long with water appearing in the blue-green colour and sometimes in Indigo- purple mesmerize the viewers. Formation of fantastic rainbow colours by hot spring water during summer and ice block mounds during winter by the water from the same spring exhibits the extreme chillness prevailing at Ladakh region (Dhar, 2008c). Very high altitude mountains of Ladakh region paves way for a unique climate - absolute dryness, severe cold, burning hot by day and piercing cold by night. Temperature in winter goes down to at least -150c to -600c and people have to fight against nature to survive. The surface link that the region has with the rest of the world* normally remains closed during the winter (Chitkara, 2002a). It explains the conditions of this frontier clod desert region. High altitude sicknesses like nose bleeding, headache and sleeplessness are common. Ladakhi is the main language of the region. Kargil, by now the famous hill range is situated at a distance of at 205 Kms from Srinagar at the height of 9000 ft. Kargil region also face extreme cold weather conditions due to mountainous terrain. The area under farming is very less, though river Suru flow through this region. Kargili is the main language of the rural folks. Though located at a very high altitude and faces extreme climatic conditions towns like Leh with orchards, groves, gardens and monasteries, Ladakh - the highest inhabitants of the world, attracts visitors from all over the globe as it located at a vantage point - Tibetan, Indian, Chinese and Islamic cultures and traditions apart from its natural beauty. The Buddhist monasteries and the barren hills are the main tourist attractions of this region. Interestingly foreign tourist outnumbers the domestic tourist's every year in this region. Important Tourist Attractions of Ladakh Division are Suru Valley, Zanskar Valley, Drass, Kargil, Lord Chamba at Wakha Mulbek, Monestry at Shergol, Hemis, Alchi, Spituk, Phyang, Shey, Lake Palace, Jama Masjid, Rangdum, Padum, Sani, Stongdey are some of the famous destination and religious important places which attract tourist towards this land of Moon.Kashmir Valley "...oh ravishingly beautiful ...".This land is more beautiful than any other I know" (Devabrantha, as quoted in Dhar, 2008d) Valley of Kashmir known as Paradise on the Earth is nestled securely at an average height of about 6000 feet above the sea level in the mighty Himalayan ranges with snow covered lofty peaks. The oval shaped valley of Kashmir spreading approximately eighty four miles in length and twenty to twenty five miles in breadth is filled with magnificent scenery at each and every inch. This small piece of land is an exquisite fairyland. There is scenery for the artist and layman, mountains for the mountaineer, flowers for the botanist, a vast field for geologist and magnificent ruins for the archaeologist (Lawrence, 2002a). In simple, the valley has everything which attracts everyone towards it. Kashmir Valley is one of the loveliest spots of the world. Against the background of lush fields, forest clad mountains, network of crystalline streams and babbling brooks, and the village look picturesque (Dhar 1998a) shows every inch of Kashmir looks beautiful. Its scenic beauty, salubrious climate, sacred shrines and hospitality nature of the people have truly made it more fascinating which cannot be explained by words for they are to be experienced at least once in lifetime. The range of mountains surrounding the Kashmir valley forms a natural guard from the outer world.

Veritable sea of mountains with the mighty Nanga Parbat (26,620 ft) in north, grim mountains with Haramukh (16,903 ft) guards the valley in east, lofty ranges Gwash Brari and the peak of Amarnath (17,321 ft), the famous pilgrim mountain guard in south, Panjal ranges with peaks of (15,000 ft) in south west, towards further north Tosh Maidan (14,000 ft) and snow covered kazi nag (12,125 ft) in the north west corner (Lawrence, 2002b) are the loyal protectors of the valley naturally. The transverse valley of Kashmir is filled with thick deposits of alluvial soil. Bordering Kashmir valley are the dry table lands with flat arid tops filled with alluvial and lacustrine material. These deposits are known as Karewas. (Husain, 2002a). These regions are difficult to be irrigated due to its elevated position.The fertile valley was submerged under water confirming this traces of old cities and its inhabitants are seen only on high cliffs and on the slope of mountains (Lawrence, 2002c). Various myths right from pre-historic times still prevail explaining the formation of Kashmir valley. Mythology reveals that Kashmir was once a lake occupied by a demon called Jalodbhava till Lord Vishnu assumed the form of a boar (varaha) struck the mountain (Varahamulla) now Baramulla, killed the demon and lake water rushed out forming Kashmir valley. Nilamata Purana, the oldest surviving Sanskrit literature of the valley reveals valley was under water, drained off by Ananta, at the behest of Vishnu. Son of Kashyapa took care of the land and named it after his father. Kalhana, in his work Rajatarangini portrays Prajapati Kashyapa killed the demon of the lake, Jalodbhava with help of Brahma, Vishnu and Shiva. The lake water was drained and named Kashmir after Kashyapa. According to Persian Chroniclers, an anonymous source material Baharistan i-Shahi (1614-25), Kashmir was under water. In its neighborhood, lived a hermit named Kash from India. In his request to God for a piece of land to pray and live, God sent three angels and the dry land so formed was named after him. According to Mulla Abdal Nabi Kashmiri, the whole world was under water and the hill of Shankaracharya summit was only visible. At this spot the throne of Soloman landed, later on it was called as Takht-i-Sulaiman. Soloman ordered his tow Jins Kashf and Mir to drain out water. Later in due recognition of their service the land formed was named as Kashfmir or Kashmir. Yet another Persian chronicle reveals Kashmir was under 'Sati Sar' meaning vast Lake. The struggle between saint kashyapa and demon of Lake Jalodbhava led to the killing of demon by Gods. When the water was drained out, the land thus formed was named as 'Kashyapa Mar' which later became 'Kashmir'. According to Nawbandhamahatmya, when the demon Jalodbhava refused to obey the command of Brahma, Vishnu and Shiva, Balabhadra (brother of

Vishnu) broke the mountain, drained the water out and Vishnu finally killed the demon. Literary reference of Dsharikaparicccheda indicates Mata sati- the consort of lord Shiva in order, to protect the people from the demon took the form of a Sharika bird. She took pebble in her beak and dropped it over the spot where the demon stayed. The pebble grew in size to a hill and the demon was crushed under its weight. The hill is known as Sharika hill after the goddess Sharika, popularly called 'Hari Prabat'. All these myths portray different version of history of Kashmir. Various versions of historical backgrounds are available for the Kashmir Valley in particular. Kalhana's 'Rajatarangani' upto AD 1006; followed by Jonarji's chronicle upto AD1420; followed by Pandit Srivara's writing upto AD1489; followed by Pragya Bhatt's 'Rajavalipatak' upto AD1586; followed by recordings of Sanskrit and Persian scholars of Mughal period as also by many English travelers (Chibber 2004) indicating Kashmir history attracted many scholars right from olden days. In the 3rd century BC, the region came under the ambit of Maurya Emperor Ashoka. The city Srinagar "city of wealth" was founded by him. Ashoka introduced Buddhism to Kashmir which was later strengthened by Kanishka. The Valley later in 530 AD gained freedom, but soon came under the rule of the Ujjain Empire. After the decline of the Vikramaditya dynasty, the valley had its own rulers. There was a synthesis of Hindu and Buddhist cultures. Buddhism thrived during 1st and 2nd centuries AD under Kushanas rule. Split between the School of Hinayana and Mahayana, the 3rd Great Buddhist Council was held in Srinagar during Kanishkas period. The split led to the eventual decline of Buddhism in the Valley, though it thrives in Ladakh region even today. In the 8th century during the rule of Lalitaditya Muktapida, Kashmir became a great kingdom extending from north India to parts of Central Asia. Famous sun (Martand) Temple, Valleys, canal irrigation system which survived for centuries were founded during his rule. The role of dynasties in Hindu Kingdoms of Kashmir was not only noteworthy but also distinctive (Kaul, 1999a). It unfolds clearly the ability of Kashmiri's in handling the state affairs efficiently. Around 12th century AD, men's with strong shoulders and standard arms invading from Central Asian areas stayed in Kashmir permanently, regrouped themselves as able and courageous soldiers, took employment under rulers of Kashmir and proved their battle worthiness even during the difficult times. Many Persians and other victims of Mongol invasions crept into the Kashmir kingdom and other areas, mingled with local population and promoted Islam by attracting and converting without any resistance from local authorities. After the death of king Odvandeva in 1338, Kashmir came under the Muslim rule in 1339. The Mughal emperor Akbar conquered it in 1587 and in 1752, it passed into the hands of Afghan rulers. Ahmad Shah Abdali, the most unpopular ruler, in the entire history of Kashmir subjected the people to suffer a lot. In 1819 with the help of the Dogra Army of Jammu, Sikh ruler of Punjab Maharaja Ranjit Singh evicted the Pathans from Kashmir. With Britisher's defeating Sikh, and later on payment of 75,00,000 Nanak Shahi currency and signing the 'Treaty of Amritsar' with East India Company in 1846, Kashmir along with other parts as mentioned in the treaty came under the rule of Maharaja Gulab Singh of Jammu. The State was governed by Dogra rulers till 1947 when Maharaja Hari Singh signed the Instrument of Accession in favour of the Indian Union on 26 October 1947. Thus all through the Kashmiris have suffered terribly from foreign subjugation and colonisation (Kaul, 1999b). It is, however, remarkable that in this long period of suppression the Kashmiris refused to be divided on the basis of religion even when the rulers tried to sow the seeds of Hindu – Muslim or Shia – Sunni feuds (Bazaz, 1998). It bears testimony to the spirit of the people of Kashmir even during the most trying times. The Kashmir valley comprises of the valleys including Liddar Valley, Extending between Anantanag and Pahalgam and surrounded by lofty mountains with dense forest the valley divides into two branches at Pahalgam. In north- eastern side it stretches up to the Sheshnag and the cave of Amarnath. The road up to Amarnath cave is traversed yearly by Hindu Pilgrims during months of July and August. River Liddar is fed with streams arising out of the kolhai and Sheshnag glaciers flows in this valley. Sind Valley, With snow covered peaks guarding either side, of the Sind Valley, it spreads over a distance of about 100 kms between Ganderbal and the Zoji-la pass. This is one of the most beautiful valleys in Kashmir valley received its name due to Sind - Lar River flowing through this valley. Sonamarg meadow and vishansar, krishnasar and Gangabal lakes attract tourists in large number every year. Lalab Valley, Situated in the north-western side of Kashmir Lalab Valley is widely known for its apple, cherry, peach and walnuts and thick deodar forest. Lahwal stream irrigates this oval shaped valley making it as an excellent grazing ground. Dense forest of deodar around the valley adds to its beauty. Lalab valley is known for the fowls called 'Khassi'. Its multi coloured feathers and very attractive physical structure resembles peacock.

Mountains are invaluable assets to the people of Kashmir Valley with their bewitching beauty, mystic spiritualism, physiographic complexity, unparallel climatic conditions, magnificent woods and enchanting lakes. Few countries can offer anything grander than the deep green mountain torn (Lawrence, 2002d). Surrounded by an unbroken ring of high mountains the lowest point in the valley has an elevation of 1600 mts and the mean elevation is 1,840 mts above the sea level. Owing to these mighty mountains the valley owes its river, streams, rain, fertility of the soil, flood and famines (Hasan, 2002a). Constantly varying in form and colour the mountain ring appear as delicate semi-transparent videt relieved against a saffron sky in the early morning, with raising sun deepens further ravines appears in purple blue and indigo, further it becomes all blue and lavender. When the sun is exactly over the head, mountain appears in richer violet and pale bronze slowly it becomes rose and pink with yellow or orange snow. Late in the evening when the sun set's it appears as a ruddy crimson with the snow spearing as a pale creamy green by contrast. It would be difficult to describe the colours that are found on the Kashmir Mountains. (Lawrence, 2002e). Unique and imposing mountains stand alongside the pleasant geography with the cold winds as a sole witness to all activities taking place in and around Kashmir valley right from pre-historic times. Mountains had direct influence on the history of Kashmir as they acts as a natural guard and protected the valley from numerous foreign invasions for a longer period. Apart from the natural beauty of the valley, agricultural prosperity of the valley depends on mountains as they provide water for irrigating lands. In Kashmir history, mountains are not simply a background, but they personify the character. Such is the beauty of the mountain range in Kashmir that any attempt to describe them lands one to struggle for words. It had a hundred faces and innumerable aspects, ever-changing, sometimes smiling, sometimes sad and full of sorrow. It was like the face of the beloved that one sees in a dream and that fades away on awakening. (Akbar, 1985). This expresses its matchless beauty.

Margs are simply open grass lands and are very charming, often prompting viewers to compare with the Alps of Switzerland. These margs attracts lot of tourists towards Kashmir Valley in large numbers due to its mesmerising beauty. Famous margs of Kashmir valley are Nagmarg, The prettiest of the Margs in Kashmir is Nagmarg. Located at the head of Wular Lake this picturesque grassy meadow land along with glassy waters of lake attracts tourists. Lovely mountains of the Kaj-i-Nag and Kaghan and the ranges of Pir Panjal are also visible from here adding beauty to this marg. These grassy lands are the favourite grazing pastures for cattle, sheep and ponies. Sonamarg, At about 90 kms away from the north-east of Srinagar located amidst forests of various trees. Sonamarg the meadow of gold is a charming and a very attractive camping garden for visitors of all ages. Colourful flowers with its wilderness make Sonamarg a lovely replica of Alps. Gulmarg, About 52 kms away in southwest of Srinagar, Gulmarg is located at a height of 8000 feet above the sea-level. With fir trees in clumps, pure water streams, a ridge of pines along with dense forest cover in slopes of mountain far behind 'Gulmarg' meaning the meadow of roses. This famous holiday spot for Northern India is half buried in snow during winter spread from June to September. The place is flocked by tourists during the season. India's premier ski resort is located here. During summer this area is occupied by huge flocks of cattle and sheep for the rich fodder. The mountain of Nanga Parbat is visible from Gulmarg. Gulmarg Gondola of the J&K State is the highest Cable car project in the world.

Another important land mark that attracts tourists from all over the world since time immemorial is the magical beauty of lakes. Owing to the beautiful mountain scenery surrounding them the Wular, the Dal and the Manasbal Lake are the most beautiful lakes in the valley region. Wular Lake, The largest fresh water lake in India nestled among lofty mountains in north-east of Kashmir valley. The lake spreads about 16 kms in length and 9.6 kms in breadth with ill-defined shores. Island made by the great Kashmiri king zain-ul-abadin and its ruins in the north-east corner of the lake convey that once upon a time it was a beautiful place. Quiet surface of rolling waves found in this lake are due to the winds and gale from mountain gorges and hills. The Bohnar, Madmati and Erin streams flow into this lake (Lawrence, 2002f) while from south the Jhelum seeks a passage through the Wular to Baramulla. This lake lies between Bandipore and Sopore at a distance of 75 kms. Dal Lake, No doubt nature has done everything possible to make Dal Lake one of the most beautiful spots on the earth. Spreading about 8 km in length and 6.4 kms in breadth, with mountain ridges, shapes and shadows reflecting in clear and soft water the Dal Lake attracts attracting visitors all around the year. It is really difficult to say when the lake is most beautiful. Perhaps in the whole world there is no corner so pleasant as the Dal Lake (Lawrence, 2002g). The Park of plane trees known as the Nasim Bagh, the garden breeze enhances the natural beauty of the lake. Each and every time the onlookers will find something new being added to its already existing exquisite beauty. The famous Mughal gardens are situated around it. Floating vegetable gardens, fields of lotus blossoms, houseboats add more to this picturesque splendor of nature. One always finds it most difficult to tear oneself away from the glorious view (Biscoe, 1998a).Manasbal Lake, Located at a distance of 29 Kms from

Srinagar, the deepest lake of Kashmir valley Lake Manasbal with Pink lilies and deep clear water adds charm to the Lake. It is 5 km. long and 1 km wide. This gentle beauty of the lake attracts visitors though Grand Mountains. This lake is not rich in natural resources. Water of Manasbal reaches the Jhelum River through a canal. The hot springs found in this lake never freeze even in the coldest winter. Harwan Lake, Situated at a distance of 21 kms from Srinagar, Harwan Lake is 278 meters long, 137 meters wide and 18 meters deep. This lake is the main source of water supply to Srinagar city. Scenic beauty of this lake attracts visitors in large numbers Hokarsar Lake, Located on the Baramulla road at about 13 kms from Srinagar, Hokarsar Lake is surrounded by Willow trees grown in abundance on its bank. The willow trees enrich the beauty of this lake in all seasons. Spreading about 5 kms in length and 1.5 kms in width, this lake is worth visiting for its scenic beauty.

Springs "Kashmir is garden of eternal springs" (Jehangir as quoted in Bamzai, 1962a) Recognized as a great sanctity for its water cold in summer and warm in winter, springs are useful auxiliaries to the mountain streams for irrigation and in some places act as source of drinking water to the people. Anantnag is well known place for countless springs. (Lawrence, 2002h). The Maliknag spring in this area is known for its sulphurous content and its water is widely known for garden cultivation. Achobal, Gushing out of the Sosanwar hill, Achobal is the most beautiful among all the springs sight from olden days. Emperor Jahangir was very much attracted towards its beauty. Verinag, Another deep blue water spring known widely for its beauty. Verinag is located at 70 kms from Srinagar is the source of Jehlum. Kokarnag, Kokarnag spring water satisfies both hunger and thirst. It is a sweet water spring. Located at about 80 kms from Srinagar near kokarnag, the pristine valley of Duksum is a wonderful camping place. The water of this spring is good and liked by all as a source of drinking water. (Hasan, 2002b). No doubt these springs are eye feast to the tourists as they throng in large numbers to these various springs for their medical values as well.

Climate "Srinagar and the Valley have a delightful climate and are far more beautiful than any hill station" (Nehru, as quoted in Parthasarathi, 1989.The climate of the valley of Kashmir has its own peculiarities. The seasons are marked with sudden change. Kashmir valley fortunately possesses an enchanting climate. (Dhar, 2008e). The valley has huge potential to attract tourists. Kashmir valley is enclosed on all sides by mountains rising to an elevation of

15,000 feet and above. This hinders the air circulation in the Kashmir Valley. Foot of Kashmir hills facing Punjab side receives heavy rainfall due to south-west monsoon and it decreases as the elevation increases towards Kashmir valley. Rains in the southern end of the valley, and northern part of Kashmir Valley were parched with drought. (Lawrence, 2002i). This shows difference in rainfall that exists in the Kashmir Valley. High mountains and unique geographical set up gives six well distinctive climatic characteristics. In spring (known locally as Sont lasts from 16 March to 15 May), the valley becomes a blanket of emerald green grass. After winter the smell, colour and beauty of the land wears a spirit of thanks giving form after a long rigorous winter. The spring season lifts the mood of Kashmiris. They flock the springs and almond-gardens with joy and pay pilgrimages. In springs showers are frequent. In summer (known locally as Retkol lasts from 16 May to 15 July), the mountains are dark blue in colour with snow capped peaks, clear streams, cool springs, beautiful lakes and pine forest. The summer season altogether makes Kashmir 'the playground of Asia'. When heat is excessive in June, heavy thunderstorms cool the air. In rainy season (known locally as Waharat lasts from 16 July to 15 September), valley receive rainfall with dark clouds touching the mighty mountains. It makes a wonderful sight for the viewers. July and August witness showers but are not frequent. In autumn (known locally as Harud lasts from 16 September to 15 November), the trees and forest in Kashmir valley turn into bronze and copper colours with foliage in golden yellow and green. This season clads the Valley in brilliant colour of gold and red. Rustling and musical sound on a walk over fallen chinar leaves makes the trip very pleasant for the visitors in this climate. In September temperature beings to fall, and the nights become cool. October and November are bracing months with pleasant sunny days and cold nights. In winter (known locally as Wandah lasts from 16 November to 15 January), Kashmir valley starts receiving snowfall making it a pleasant and memorable season for those who are interested in viewing snowfall. In December clouds will appear and by the end of December heavy snowfall will start. In winter the Valley is silent with white mantle of snow covering its entire surface. In Ice Cold season (known locally as Sishur lasts from 16 January to 15 March), the entire land is covered with snow. Intense cold makes winter a very harsh climate for common people and animals as they face a lot of hardships with snowfalls, frozen lakes, freezing rivers. Thus, Kashmir valley in hard winter is like a huge refrigerator (Lawrence, 2002j). Intense cold prevails till February. Earlier men left Kashmir for the six months of winter, when it was occupied by peshachas (demons) (Hassnain,

2002b) portrays the severe climatic condition of Kashmir Valley. None of the tourists to Kashmir Valley is left unimpressed by the grandeur of the romantic scenery, lovely serpentine rivers, evergreen forests, unending white sheets of snow in winter, colourful and fragrant flowers and tasty fruits of summer. It is very difficult for anyone to identify which is the Kashmir's best season. The older people often feel that the climate is changing and believe the valley receives very less snow fall, of late. Canals are dry, springs are decreasing, climate in general is becoming dry as that of in Punjab. Though it is also true, Kashmir valley presents an unparalleled climatic condition, physiographic complexity and extremes. (Chitkara, 2002b) It is the charming, unique and distinct climatic condition of the Kashmir valley that attracts tourists from all parts of the globe even in present day.

Inhabitants "...it is the people of this place who realize the value of peace and have a deep yearning for the same" (Baba, 2002). Kashmir consists of numerous ethnic and cultural groups. Kashmiris are early immigrants from India. Traces of Aryans in India is found in Kashmir (Dhar, 2008f) explains the existence of people from olden days. Kashmiris made remarkable contribution to Sanskrit literature, mystical poetry, the shaiva philosophy, grammar and the sciences. Thus the intellectual capabilities of Kashmiris are well established. Blend of various cultures is found among Kashmiris as they had contact with Roman, Greek and Persian civilizations. Hinduism and Buddhism coexisted during the olden days. Having bestowed with such beautiful land, people of Kashmir, if left uninterrupted, would have continued contributing much more to the art and architecture. Unfortunately, Kashmiris never enjoyed peace. Despite achieving laurels in other fields, Kashmiris are unable to design an efficient political systems and continuous suppression and oppression by the invaders, they lost the glorious traditions of safeguarding their homeland. Many cruel invaders forced their way into the valley resulting in ethnic infiltration and conversion though the Chaks, Pathans, Mughals and Sikhs during their respective rule. They tried their best to alter but none of them succeeded in altering the unique and special character of the people. The basic fabric of Kashmiri culture still remains intact due to their patience, perseverance, sense of sufferance and maneuvering genius. The influence of Dards, ladakhis, Punjabis Shiks, Rajputs, Gujjars has also moulded the cultural ethos of the Kashmiris (Husain, 2002c). They will patiently endure and suffer, but will not fight (Biscoe, 1998b). Kashmiris on the whole are non-aggressive. God-fearing and temperate, have good physique but lack good muscles. Wordly warfare never ends into hitting each other. (Dhar,

2008g) It amplifies the peace loving nature of Kashmiris. In spite of his great physical strength and powers of endurance, the Kashmiri is highly strung and neurotic and he will often weep on slight provocation (Neve, 1998). Thus Kashmiris in general are very soft natured. Though Kashmiris are a bundle of contradictions with positive and negative elements found equally in their character, they are extremely warm, friendly and very hospitable in nature. They tend to over feed the guest and pay lavish attention to satisfy them. About ninety percent of the population in valley follows Islam of both Sunni and Shia sects, rest are Kashmiri Pandit and Sikhs. Professing different faiths - Islam, Hinduism, and Buddhism – the three religious sub communities of Kashmir historically have lived in peace with one another. (Ganguly & Bajpai, 1994) This indicates the accommodative nature of the people in earlier times. Kashmiri Muslims men wear pheran, a long loose gown, a white turban tied on a skull cap, Shalwar and lace less shoes called gurgabi. Kashmiri Muslim women wear pheran of knee-length, loose and embroidered in front and on the edges. Now a day's shalwar - kameez is used widely but pheran is more attractive than modern shalwar- kameez. Muslim women also wear bunches of earrings with thick silver chain to support its weight. They use the head gear, the kasaba with an overhanging pin-scarf that falls gracefully over the shoulders. Unmarried Muslim girls wear skull caps, embroidered with gold thread and embellished with silver pendants, trinkets and amulets. Kashmiri Hindu men wear churidar pyjama instead of a shalwar. Kashmiri pandits are very simple, tend to be individualistic, high in self-esteem and largely intellectual. There is scarcely any thing which he cannot do. (Dhar, 2008h). This reveals they are good in doing everything. Kashmiri Hindu women wear pheran which touches her feet. The head gear taranga is tied to a hanging bonnet and tapers down to the heels from behind. They are very fond of jewellery which is widely seen in their head gear, ears, necks and arms glisten with ornaments. Married women wear dejharoo, a pair of gold pendants, hanging on a silk or golden thread passing through the holes in the ears pierced at the top end of the lobes. The tea Kashmiris drink in kahva made up of green tea leaves, brewed in the samovar, enriched with almonds, cardamom seeds, cinnamon stalks, and sugar but without milk. They also take other kinds of tea shirchai-salted and milked, pink in colour, with lot of cream on top of it. Rice is the staple food of the Kashmiris. They enjoy karam sag (leafy vegetable) nadru (lotus stalk) and turnips in general. They also enjoy lamb dishes in various ways, each distinct in the taste from the other. During winter Kashmiris consume dried and preserved vegetables known as Hokshuns. During summers, they dry vegetables and hang them on house walls. To overcome shortage of fresh vegetable supplies in winter due to lack of transportation, they use these dry vegetables. Kashmiris are slowly changing due to the impact of modern influences. Yet they preserve their own custom and traditions. Though, there are changes, still it is their hospitality coupled with the natural beauty of the place that attracts the tourist to this glorious land.

Kashmiriyat "Kashmir thus became even more so than the rest of India, a laboratory for this process of the blending of cultures" (Bamzai, 1962b). Besides its natural beauty, Kashmir Valley is also known for its unique cultural ethos which has evolved through centuries in a seamless co-existence called as Kashmiriyat. Hindus and Muslims are much attracted towards the teachings of Rishis and Sufi Pirs. The impact of the preaching's on their culture is visible even today. With the advent of Sufism and Rishism, shrine worship became a common feature providing a unique platform to build bridges between people of different faiths. Numerous Sufi shrines still attract devotees both Hindus and Muslims. They pay their respects to the saints who preached religious tolerance and contributed significantly to the evolution of Kashmiriyat. People from all walks of life and all shades of opinion took inspiration and guidance from Sheikh Noorudin Noorani, the greatest Sufi Saint of Kashmir. This great philosopher brought a religious, political, social, and cultural transformation by spreading the message of tolerance, vegetarianism, and communal peace among the people of Kashmir Valley. Kashmiriyat is a synthesis of the great traditions of different religions. Various Sufi Saints of Kashmir thus contributed remarkably to the development of its composite culture. Tolerance and helping attitude have always been a way of life in Kashmir. This particular disposition of the people made them the most admirable in the world right from the olden days.

Kashmiri Language "... both Kashmiri Hindus and Muslims have identified Kashmiri as their mother tongue" (Bhatt & Bhargava 2005a). Kashmir has been the home of Sanskrit learning right from the olden days. The idyllic surroundings of the Valley provided a congenial soil for the growth of Sanskrit (Dhar, 2008i). Famous travelers like Hiuen T Sang and Ou – Kong visited Kashmir to study Sanskrit text. With the advent of Islam, Kashmiri scholars and government officials started learning Persian language. Sooner Kashmiri became practically a spoken language, and the Sharda script slowly lost its importance. People inhabiting the Kashmir Valley speak Kashmiri – the most important language of the state. It is also one of the *recognized regional languages of Indian union. The Kashmiri's live in a land where beauties of nature are abundant which excite the imagination of the Kashmiri as a result of which this land produced great poet and poetesse (Dhar, 1998b). This implies that nature paved way for literature in Kashmir. Lalleshwari's contributions, Nand Rishi's Nur – Nama, Habba Kuttan songs even today echoes in the Kashmir Valley. Arnimal, Mahmud Gami, Rasul Mir, Parmanand, Ghulam Ahmad Mahjoor, Abdul Ahad Azad, Abdul Sattar Asi, Zinda Kaul, Dina Nath Nadim, and Mirza Arif contributed immensely to the literary works and left indelible mark on Kashmiri literature which inspired subsequent generations. The Jammu and Kashmiri Academy of Art, Culture, and Languages established in October 1958 is the apex body that fosters of Kashmiri and other languages of the region further.*

Dance, Drama and Music "But with the decay of Sanskrit learning the Kashmiris characteristic love of history and tradition did not wane and wither away" (Kak, 1998). Various fine arts exponents by Udbhatta, Lollabata, Sankuka, and Bhatta Nayaka are conversant with Bharata's Natyashastra. Kashmiri classical dance style had a religious background and artistes ably depicted the vast range of human emotions through their art (Dhar, 2008j). Ballet dancing and Choral music are played by artists during the period of king Kalasa (1063 – 89 A.D). Dancers maintained a high standard of art and even achieved the status of courtiers during the rule of Harsha (1089 – 1101 A.D). Classical dancers performed at the court of Sultan Zian – Ul – Abidin (1420 – 70 A.D). It shows the support and patronage provided to artists. Mughal rulers used to watch dance performances in the gardens. The artists used to sing in Persian, widely called as 'hafizas', enriched with musical instruments such as Santoor, Soz, Tabla, etc. Kashmiri Folk-Songs and Folk-Dances and dances like Ruf, Dambaeli accompanied with musical instruments express the wisdom of ages, culture and tradition of Kashmiri people even today. Bhand Pather is a well known traditional folk style combining play and dance in a satirical style where social traditions, eveils are performed in various social and cultural functions. References to theatrical performances, stage setup, band players, dresses used by the artists were found in Rajatarangini shows the drama staged by the artists in ancient times. On festival occasions artists and band players received gifts from nobles and kings. Plays like Zaina Vilas, Zaina Charitha, Vikrama Charitha, and Banaswara Vadh were some of the famous plays staged during ancient and medieval periods in Kashmir. In the modern days few dramatic clubs were formed which enacted the plays of Agha Hashar and Betab. After the formation of National Cultural

Front plays like Greesi Sund Ghara and Batahar attracted thousands of audiences. Drama exhibits tradition and culture of Kashmiri even today. Music was a part of fine art in ancient Kashmir. It was an essential component at religious worships and in the courts of kings and high nobles. Kashmiri music is a blend of both Indian and Persian prototypes and evolved Sufiana Kalam with Forty – four modes which have Indian as well as Persian names. Lute, Flute, Drum were common musical instruments. Various musical instruments are made up of earthen pots and brass vessels. Santoor popularly known as Sitar with a 100 strings is very famous among all musical instruments of Kashmir. Sufiana Music introduced in the 15th century in Kashmir by Iran became the classical music form of Kashmir with a good fusion of Indian Ragas. Santoor, Sitar, Kashmiri Saz, Wasool or Tabala are the most widely used instruments by the performers. It is disheartening to note that only very few are practicing this classical music in Kashmir now. Art, Architecture and Handicraft "How beautiful are the articles made by the deft fingers of Kashmiri's workers! To look at them was a pleasure, to handle them a delight" (Dhar, 1940).Kashmiri's artistic qualities made them excel in art and over the years entered into its own style known as Kashmiri Qalam. Though medieval artists were interested in wall paintings or murals, later Kashmiri artists were influenced by the painters of Basohli and Kangra. The few available pieces prove their interest in art right from the olden days. Impressive remains of stone architecture across the length and breadth of Kashmir Valley with lofty pyramidal roofs acting as a barrier against heavy snow and rains reveal the unique features of ancient Kashmiri architecture and the skill in building massive structures. Influence of Roman and Greek styles are also found in Kashmiri architecture which makes it distinct from the Hindu architecture of the rest of India. Martand 'the architectural lion of Kashmir' exhibits the dignity and solidarity though it is in remnants. Avantisvami – Vishnu temple built by Avantivarman at Avantipur and the temples of the Sugandhesa and the Samkara – Gaurisvara built by Sankaravarman though in ruins reveals the awe inspiring classical design. Decline in Kashmiri style of architecture began from the 10th century B.C. Political instability made people to forget the art of stone architecture in Kashmir Valley. Wooden architecture in Kashmir with decorative motifs and the Arab concept of spaciousness are closely associated with Muslim architecture. The mosque of Mian Sahib built by Zian –ul- Abidin is well known for its tile decoration even today. Khanqah mosque of Shah Hamdan in Srinagar, on the banks of Jhelum River is a wonderful example for medieval style of Kashmiri's Muslim architecture. Kashmir's wood carver's best craftsmanship is visible from the doors and windows of mosque Shah Hamdan. Jama Masjid of Srinagar is also a best example of Kashmir wooden structure. The Pathar Masjid (stone mosque) built by Nur Jahan in 1623 A.D. under the supervision of Malik Haider Chaudhury with local grey lime stone comprising nine arches, revolutionised the Kashmiri architecture. Hazratbal mosque built during the period of Emperor Shah Jahan is a blend of Kashmir and Mughal architecture. Landscaping and gardening are the two important traditional passions of early Hindus and Buddhists. Mughals, later became world famous for their obsession for beauty followed the same traditions. Jehangir during his rule laid out world famous gardens at Nishant, Shalimar, Achabal, and Verinag. Later Shah Jahan improved them and built small pleasure garden around the spring at Chashma Shahi. In general Kashmiri architecture reveals influences of various religions. It stands unique even today illuminating how craftsmen excelled in his own talent. Apart from scenic beauty and bracing climate Kashmir is a shopper's paradise especially for handicrafts. Few places in earth can offer such a rich variety of artifacts. Excellence in weaving, unique colours, lovely design, and involved workmanship - all made Kashmiri handicrafts famous in the global markets right from olden days. There is hardly anything, you discover, that a Kashmiri craftsman will not do well, once he gets down to it (Milne, 1998). This exposes the true spirit of craftsmanship hidden in Kashmiri. Kashmir carpets in both wool and silk, papier – mache, wooden furniture and accessories, stone jewellery boxes, woolen shawls, crewel embroidery, stone work, silver work, namda and many more are a lifetime investment for the consumers.

Kashmir carpets, The hand-woven pile carpet is the national craft of Kashmir. The carpet industry, introduced into the Valley by Sultan Zain-ul-Abidin is now one of the leading industries of Kashmir. Smooth-faced and pile carpets with floral and other designs is a fine example of Kashmir's diverse cultural diversity. Kashmir shawls, are world famous for their quality wool, colour and design. The fabric called pashimina is woven into shawl either in loom or by embroidery. Price of these shawls depends upon the design and time taken for production. Embroidery, Kasida is the world-famous embroidery of Kashmir. Embroidered on shawls or saris, by the craftsman is a must buy as a souvenir item of the place. Papier Mache, Products are beautifully painted over with various designs of ornamental patterns which make the product more appealing. Wood carving, Wood carving is the famous cottage industry of Kashmir Valley. Chairs, cabinets, writing or dining tables, jewellery boxes and ornamental caskets, walnut wood products such as - cigar boxes and trays, table-tops, handkerchief and collar boxes are delicately carved with floral designs exhibiting the craftsmanship. Namda, This is a warm, colourful, and inexpensive floor covering made out of pressed felt. Rectangular, oval or round, embroided in chain stich are liked by customers. Metal Work, Extremely beautiful metal work is found in Kashmir with chinar and lotus leaf designs. Samovars tea – kettle of Russian origin is an excellent example of Kashmiri artisan. Kangri, The Kashmiri chafing vessel, its earthen bowl encased in wickerwork is the source of heat during extreme winter. The traditional Kangri of Chari Shrief is very famous for its design and durability. Khatam-Bandi, Any description of Kashmiri woodwork is not complete without mentioning about this Khatam – Band. Panels of pine wood are cut into different geometrical shapes and used for ceilings of rooms. This sort of decoration is found in the house boats of Kashmir.

Kashmir Valley abounds in rich flora and fauna mainly due to its geographical location and climatic conditions. This land is covered with tall green trees and houses a wide variety of vegetation which add colour to its physical beauty. Trees look in different colours in different seasons, They give a breathtaking look during autumn, which attracts lot of visitors to the Valley. Chinar is the most magnificent of the Kashmir trees and is the found throughout the valley. It grows too tall and is of much use to the people of Kashmir. Apart from Chinar, trees like Walnut, Willow, Almond and Cider also forms the rich flora of Kashmir. Kashmir Valley is very famous for Willow Wood which is mainly used for making cricket bat. Mountainous region in the state are covered with dense deodar, fir and pine trees. Nestled between the mountain ranges, Kashmir Valley has rich variety of flora. There are about 3,300 species of flowering plants found in Kashmir Valley. Kashmir Valley is also known for various medical herbs which are very rare to find in other parts of the world. Numerous medical herbs found here are used in unnani system of medicine. Owing to the distinct topography and climate the region has a variety of species. World famous saffron is pride of Kashmir Valley. Purple colour flowers appearing just above the ground itself add beauty and aroma to the region. It reaps huge profit to the people. Pampur and Budgam are the main regions of the valley cultivate saffron. This is also called as Cultivated Gold. Kashmir has been the symbol of fruits and flowers right from the olden days. The age-old traditional fruit cultivation has widely coloured the serenity and tranquility of valley's landscape. Apples, Cherry, Peaches, Apricot, Strawberry, and Plums of different varieties are grown in Kashmir Valley. Forest and Wildlife "Almost all the mountains are coated *with dense forests, which besides lending charm and healthful fragrance to the atmosphere, are a great factor of revenue to the country" (Bhatt & Bhargava 2005b).Jammu and Kashmir is the northernmost state of India, surrounded by mountains on all sides Kashmir Valley is rich in forest wealth and has unique wild animals and birds attracting travelers to the Valley. Of the total 15,948 Sq Kms, of the Valley forest area spreads over 8,128 Sq Kms covering 50. 96 % of total area of Kashmir Valley. Forests are covered by tall and wide variety of trees along with a wide variety of bushes. In different seasons they appear in different colours adding beauty to the Kashmir Valley. Wildlife Sanctuaries located in this valley are Dachingam National Park (Srinagar) and Gulmarg Biosphere Reserve (Baramulla). One - third of world's mammalian species especially mountain animals are present in Kashmir. Topography, climate, and vegetation are the main reasons for inhabitation of such large variety of species of wildlife. The wild mammals, namely Kashmir stag, Himalayan Black and Brown Bear, Musk Deer, Himalayan Marmot and leopard are the special attractions to the travelers. Kashmir Stag 'Hangul' an endangered species is found in Dachigam Wildlife Sanctuary, Srinagar. It is brownish red in colour. However the colour depends upon season and the age of 'Hangul'. These wild deer are also found in Wardwan, Gurez Valley. Snow Leopards are found in high altitude region of above 3,200 mts Covered with thick coat of fur silver colour with black spots, they are found in pine forest and in grassy meadows for prey in winter. In the summer, they remain in snow covered areas. These primary predators are good climbers and efficient stalkers normally hunt in night and therefore less visible in the day light. Mountain goats, Musk Deer, Ibex, Monkey, and Lingers are also seen in the forest region of Kashmir. Varieties of rare birds are seen in Kashmir Valley. Nearly 187 species of breeding birds and 42 species of fishes are found in the Valley. The Black Necked Crane is a rare species of crane found in Kashmir Valley apart from Tibet and China. They bond for life and the courtship dance of the crane is a wonderful sight for the visitors.*

Fairs and festivals are an integral part of Kashmiris life, though the Valley is dominated by Muslim population fairs and festivals of other religions are also celebrated with the same spirit. Rich and deep rooted ancient culture of Kashmir is revealed in such fairs and festivals celebrated by the people of Kashmir even today. Bara Wafat and Shab-e-Meraj are two great events in the life of the Kashmiri Muslims. Urs-e-Shah Hamdan, Urs-e-Pir Dastgir, Urs-e-Rafimal, Urs-e-Baba Rishi, and Urs-e-Naqshband are celebrated in shrines. The Shiite Muslims observe Moharram, Id-e-Ghadir, and Nauroz, a festival of harvest season. Pat fair of Bhaderwah is celebrated in remembrance of Raja Nagpal with pageant of 'pat' taken amidst dance and drums every year. Mughal Emperor Akbar decided to manhandle and punish the Raja for his arrogance of passing his legs first, instead of bowing his head while entering the court. It turned out to be impossible for Akbar to punish the Raja, as Raja's patron deity Vasaknag, a snake having five heads attacked the soldiers whenever they tried to capture the Raja. Kapalmocham Festival celebrated in the village Degam in which people perform Shradas of their minor deceased children by giving away clothes and utensils. Jwalamukhi fair is celebrated on 16th July every year in the village Khrew near Pulwama. Hundreds of stalls selling different commodities are set up by Muslim peasants which bear testimony to the unity of the people of Kashmir. Tulip festival celebrated in the month of April in Asia's largest tulip garden, Siraz Bagh, Srinagar. People arrive in large number to have a glimpse of rich and varied colours of Tulip during this festival. Spring Festival also called as harvest festival is celebrated in the month of April. This festival is marked by numerous fairs. Cherry Festival is celebrated in the month of May. Competitions are held among Cherry Growers and varieties of Cherry could be purchased in this festival. Arts & Crafts Festival held in the month of May by the side of Nageen Lake showcases the rich handicrafts of Kashmir Valley. Shikara Festival held in the month of May in Dal Lake. Traditional Kashmiri boat rides are conducted in colourful manner amidst lotus and colourful floating vegetable markets. Kheer Bhawani Festival Maha Yagna conducted during this festival attracts large number of devotees and different of commodities are sold in stalls in this festival. Gurez Festival conducted in unexplored Gurez Valley in the month of July attracts many tourists. Rafting camps, dances and folk songs are performed by school children and local performers with great enthusiasm. Water Sports Festival held in the month of July in Nageen, Manasbal, and Dal Lake hosts water skiing, boat races, water scooter rides which attract young adventure water sports lovers. Garden of Paradise Festival The famous Mughal Garden is the venue for this festival. Cultural events, food stalls add more colour to this terraced garden especially in the month of August. Apple Festival celebrated across Kashmir in the month of September attracts visitors in large numbers for the show where delicious and colourful apples are displayed. Apple is called as treasure of Kashmir and competition is held for apple growers in this festival. Saffron Festival World famous Saffron is found in Kashmir. Varieties of saffron can be purchased here. Cultural programmes and Kashmir Cuisine are other attractions of this fair. Kashmir Snow Festival is held in the month of December in Gulmarg and various winter sports for sports lovers are organised. Cultural events conducted by artists add more delight to this festival.

Other Major Man Made Attractions in Kashmir Valley "Another important branch of architecture in which the Mughals excelled, and in which they left their mark upon Srinagar is gardening" (Kak, 2002). Kashmir valley's enchanting beauty has won praise from wide range of visitors since time immemorial. Apart from its natural beauty, the valley is a unique place in the world where various people contributed their craftsmanship exhibiting their skills and add further beauty to this lake doted valley. Tourists even today stand mesmerized by such works. Kashmir valley tourist attractions will remain incomplete without mentioning such works. A brief description of the man made attractions of Kashmir Valley includes Cheshma Shahi, This is the famous garden near the Dal Lake, raised in 1632 by Ali Mardan Khan, the Governor of Kashmir during the regime of Emperor Shahjahan. This garden though small in size has two terraces separated from each other by a height of 18 feet. The fountains, water channels and reservoirs which are visible even today were built when the garden was originally constructed. It was renovated from time to time and old balconies were reconstructed. Spreading about 80 hectares this garden houses 1.5 lakh ornamental plants. The beauty of the garden attracts tourists from all over the world. Nishant Garden, Located at the foot hills of Zabarwan hills bordering Dal Lake spreads over 50 acres. The garden, offers a magnificent view across the whole of Dal Lake. Comprising 10 terraces with lawns of flowers, fountains and waterfalls along with chinar tress exhibit the beauty of the garden. Pari Mahal, Mainly used as a school of astrology, was built by Prince Dara Shikoh for his tutor Mullah Shah. Though, it was ruined with passage of time, this was renovated and reconstructed by the State Government and a beautiful garden was also laid around it. Shalimar Garden: Ancient history out Raja Parvarsen built a dignified building with paintings and drawings for the comfortable stay of Saint Sogram Swami. Later in 1629, emperor Jehangir built a beautiful garden at the site which was given the name Shalimar meaning 'beautiful house'. Covering an area of 12 40 78 hectares this garden is a delight to tourists. In the summer light and music show, plays related to Mughal Emperors are organized by the tourism department Nishant Park, Located at the south-east of Bandipore town facing the Wular Lake this garden attracts tourist in all seasons. Spreading over an area of about 20 hectares this park is treat to visitors'. This park is extended gradually in order to meet the growing number of visitors. Flower beds, ponds and Mughal type fountains, lush green ornamental trees add beauty to the garden in all seasons. Salsabeel Park, Widely known for its cold and lucid water springs located in Bandipore, park surrounding was constructed in 1963. Western area of the park is filled with lush green turf and flower beds. On the north- eastern side of the park, a mosque was also constructed. Though this park was damaged in fire, after its renovation this park emerged as the most sought attraction. This is also a famous religious and recreation centre. Harwan, Located in Srinagar, this huge garden has a beautiful canal running in the middle surrounded by flowerbeds and tall Chinar Trees. In order to maintain the natural beauty of the garden, artificially created fountains are not developed. It looks like a vast green carpet spread on the floor. This is an ideal place for picnic and excursions. This is the starting point of Dachi Gam Wildlife Sanctuary and trekking of the Mahadev Mountain starts from this point. Siraj Bagh, Located between Nehru Memorial Botanical Garden and Cheshma Shahi this garden boasts of 1, 00,000 Tulips which attract tourists during seasons. This is one of Asia's largest Tulip Gardens. Achaba, Located at the foot hill and surrounded by mighty Chinar trees, this is really a visual delight. Ornamental shrubs, sparkling fountains, and terraces make this a wonderful place to visit. Tourist bungalows and restaurants at this place make the visit more comfortable. Watlab, Located near Wular Lake, Watlab houses the Shrine of a Muslim mystic Baba Shukardin on the hill top. From here, one can see the colourful areas of Kashmir Villages. Forest Rest House at the center of the sprawling apple gardens attract tourists from all over the world. House Boats and Shikaras, Earlier Britisher's had no right to live on land in Kashmir. House boats were mainly constructed for them to stay. Later, they improvised these water dwellings on the lakes of Kashmir in the year 1888. These boats are common in Dal Lake, Nagin Lake and in Jhelum River. Traders' use small Shikaras to carry the household items, vegetables, tourists to house boat located at far off places from the shore of the Dal Lake. These House Boats are well decorated and well furnished for comfortable stay. Now a day's lot of facilities is provided in the house boats to attract the foreign tourists all round the year. Advance reservations are possible through websites. Nehru Park, Built in memory of Jawaharlal Nehru at the foot of Shankaracharya Hills is the main fun centre of Dal Lake. It attracts people of all age groups especially for evening walks and exercise. The illumination at night is the main attraction for the tourists. Hari Parbat, For Located like a crown at the Peak of Hari Parbat Hill, this fort though lost its earlier glory still stands impressive attracting visitors interested in ancient buildings.

This fort stands today as it was developed by an Afghan Governor, Atta Mohammad Khan in the 18th century. When illuminated in night with light, it is a wonderful sight. SPS Museum, Located at the left bank of the river Jhelum in Srinagar, SPS Museum is named after Sri Pratap Singh. This was developed by General Raja Sir Amar Singh and Captain S. H. Godmerry, an European scholar to exhibits rare artefacts from the region of Jammu, Kashmir, Baltistan, and Gilgit. This museum exhibits numismatics and manuscripts, weapons and utensils, furniture and decorative items, sculptures, tiles, miniature paintings, musical instruments, textiles and carpets. A visit to this museum will helps us to understand more about the region. Gulmarg Ski Resort, Housing the premier Ski Resort Gulmarg is a world famous destination for winter sport lovers. During 1998, Gulmarg hosted the first National Winter Games of India. First phase of the Gulmarg Gondola Cable Car was developed during this period. Trained instructors and equipment are available for sports persons. Camp fires and snowman around the areas are the main attraction to the tourists apart from highest lift – served Ski resort in the world providing a 80 downhill ski run of 5.2 Kms from a height of 14,000 feet in Apharwat range. Heli - Skiing also attracts tourists from faraway places. Tulip Garden: Spreads over 30 hectare nearby world famous Dal Lake. This garden is filled with 12 lakh tulip bulbs of 68 varieties of different colours present really a breath taking view. This garden has become recent tourist attraction.

Important Pilgrimage Centre in Kashmir Valley, Kashmir Valley is known for its cultural uniqueness right from the olden days. Numerous pilgrimage centre are located all over the Valley. Some of the important places that attract tourist are Hazratba, The most sacred of shrines in Kashmir Valley is Hazratbal. This shrine houses a single hair of the Prophet Mohamad (saw) brought thousands of years ago from Medina. Paved with stones and tall Chinar trees, the shrine has a distinct aesthetic appeal. Located on the west bank of Dal Lake, this shrine attracts devotees from all over the country. Charari Sharief, to honour the wisdom of Sheikh Nur –ud –din, this three tiered roof shrine supported by wooden pillars was built. Located at a distance of 28 Kms from Srinagar, People of all faith visit this shrine. Shankaracharya Temple, Located at south east of Srinagar, built on a high octagonal plinth with side walls and steps the main shrine is circular in shape. The antiquity of Shankaracharya, dedicated to Lord Shiva dates back to 200 BC. This temple attracts tourist from all over the country. Pandrethan, This is the old capital of Kashmir in the 3rd century BC. Buddhist Stupas and a Buddhist monastery are uncovered in this region. Jami Masjid, This is the largest of all

Kashmir Mosques. Though damaged by fire and rebuilt many times, it was renovated in 1961. Four minars and eight wooden columns as support add attraction to this architectural beauty. Shri Amarnath Cave: Holiest of all Hindu shrines, Amarnath is located at a distance of 141 Kms from Srinagar and about 45 Kms from Pahalgam. Trekking is the only option to reach this pilgrimage centre. Amarnath yatra is generally undertaken in July – August every year. Thousands of devotees visit this site on pilgrimage every year. Kashmir Valley has many pilgrimage places. A detailed description of all such places is beyond the scope of this thesis. As such, only important pilgrimage centers are described in brief.

Kashmir Valley Tourism through Ages, Kashmir Valley is a unique place in the world. There is hardly anyone who is left unimpressed by the romantic scenery of mountain – grit Kashmir Valley right from the olden days. Words of Hiuen T Sang, Kalhana, Alberuni, Jehangir, Thevenot, Francois Bernier, Hyppolyte Desideri, William Moorecroft, James Gilbren Gerard, Victor Jacquement, G. T. Vigne, C. R. Tollemache, Charles Hugel, and other travelers vouch for Kashmir Valley's bewitching and enchanting beauty. Kashmir Valley is the loveliest part of the globe. Kashmir's scenic beauty, salubrious climate in different seasons, snowy landscape, vast lakes, historical monuments, orchards, health resorts, monasteries, shrines, serpentine rivers, ever green forest, colourful and attractive flowers and hospitality nature of the people of the Kashmir Valley attract millions of tourists to the Valley.

Each and every inch of the Kashmir Valley is covered by scenic beauty throughout the year. With colourful flowers blossoming in the mid March to April end, fruit laden trees with colourful flowers carpeting the Valley in May and June, clear water streams and rivers providing scope for swimming, sun bathing, trekking in June and July, showers in August and September make fishing and other activities a memorable experience. Magnificent mountain tops covered with snow from mid October, water sporting from November to March, with arts, and handicrafts, in all the seasons truly makes Kashmir Valley a year round destination for all types of tourists for one or the other reasons. Srinagar in Kashmir Valley is well connected to New Delhi and other major cities in India by air and road transport network. All major airlines operate regular daily flights to Srinagar. Sheikh Ul Alam Airport located at about 12 Kms from Srinagar plays an important role in terms of air connectivity. It is an international airport with a huge capacity to handle heavy passenger traffic. The civil enclave at Srinagar Airport was established in 1979 for facilitation of civil passengers. Though the airport is situated at 5435 feet above mean sea level, it is provided with all ultra modern facilities. The peak hour capacity of the terminal building has been upgraded from 500 passengers to 950 passengers. Srinagar has a wide variety of accommodation. Deluxe hotels, guest houses, and houseboats are very famous among tourists visiting Kashmir Valley. Cottages and bungalows are available at Srinagar, Pahalgam, and in Gulmarg providing comfortable stay at reasonable price. Though hotel rooms are available as per tourist's requirement, house boats play a unique role in attracting tourists towards Kashmir valley. Various categories of house boats at Kashmir Valley provide accommodation facilities to tourists of all categories. With good air and road connectivity, adequate accommodation facilities and a salubrious climate, no wonder that Srinagar became the hub of Kashmir Valley tourism. Hub – and – Spoke itineraries are quiet common where tourists base themselves in a particular destination and take side trips to other destinations (Mc Kercher & Lew, 2004).

Valley the paradise on earth is an important destination for domestic and international tourists. Rich culture, traditions, arts, crafts, architecture, hospitality nature of Kashmiri people attracted tourist from olden days. Tourists flocked valley till 1988 and then the situation changed with the appearance of terrorism. Terror attacks resulted in downfall of tourists at Kashmir Valley. In depth understanding of problem involved in reducing the domestic tourist inflow towards Kashmir Valley is vital before designing measures to put tourism industry back on the track at Kashmir Valley. As such, it has become imperative to look deeply into the causes responsible for the growth of terrorism that casted ill effect on tourism.

AN OVERVIEW OF RELATED

LITERATURE

At the early stage of the present exercise, an attempt was made to highlight the ideas and views of eminent scholars in the two fields of terrorism and tourism through a thorough review of the relevant literature. There have been a number of studies on these subjects worldwide and with a particular reference to Jammu and Kashmir. Social scientists, defence analysts, tourism experts, top brass of defence services especially after retirement, counter terrorism specialists and peace researchers have been attentive to the problems of their concerned areas over a period of time reflecting their views, experiences and thoughts to overcome the challenges thrown by terrorism.

Friedland & Merari, (1985) while presenting the results of a public opinion survey conducted on an Israeli national sample, which was designed to evaluate the psychological impact of terrorist activity found terrorism, as a form of psychological warfare. Though terrorism activities induced fear far exceeds the actual damage, it has failed to produce the change in attitudes sought by the perpetrators of terror. Terror tactics can be effective to bring expected political changes when the actual or perceived threat exceeds certain critical level. Below this level it appears to pave the way for hardening of attitudes and strengthen opposition to the cause of terrorism. Counter terrorist action must consider factors such as public attitude towards the terrorist's goals, public reaction towards foreign terrorists, and response to internal terrorists. Though counter measures not affecting bystanders received a high degree of support, public resolve to withstand terroristic pressure depends upon effective counter terrorist measures, or the degree to which concessions are provided to terrorists and their outcome.

Singh, (1986) while estimating strengths and weaknesses of India, identifies internal unrest due to encouragement to terrorism, China's support to Pakistan, Pakistan's nuclear capabilities, poor communications and inadequate infrastructure in far flung areas and illiteracy as crucial issues which the country faces. Author views peace without strength as incorrect policy and supports the need for a strong force to deter any threat including the use of nuclear weapon of our neighbour. Understanding local population and winning their heart and mind is an appropriate solution to terrorism and re-orientation in the deployment of security forces against terrorism will curtail expenditure in combating terrorism.

Kishore, (1987) adopted functionalist approach as the structure of the government and societies by and large remains the same, argues that language and religion apart from social inequalities and regional disparities are the main issues confronting national integration in India. As no rigid principle can be applied for national integration, the author recommends to chalk out a plan depending upon the problem with due consideration to time and place apart from development, communication and education as vital tools for strengthening the national integration in India.

Uberoy, (1989) elaborating the approaches to Anti-Terrorism opines that terror strike are carried out with intention to control target area and this increases expenditure of Government towards safety and security. Democratic countries in particular face severity of the problem in combating terrorism as general public react sharpely towards strategies adopted to eliminate terrorism. In-depth focusing, utilising all resources, well balanced approaches towards effective discernment about the dimensions of the movement, containment to check the growth of all aspects of a movement, isolation of the elements or forces supporting the movement both at physical as well as psychological level and elimination for final liquidation of the movement help in controlling the complex situation. Constant and simultaneous adoptions along with the resolve, soft approaches, society involvement are required to break the cohesiveness of the terror organisation. Retaliation to deal with cross border terrorism and tracing root causes for terrorism and solving it will reduce domestic terrorism. The author strongly supports the formation of an apex body to ensure all agencies entrusted in combating terrorism are dealing with the assigned task with utmost care.

Sinclair & Stabler, (1997) vividly describe consumption of tourism product will be affected due to social unrest at a particular destination and alteration in social context can bring in changes in the pattern of tourism consumption. Strategic policies, if initiated by government may help to alter the market structure generating more positive output from tourism. Focused research, investigation of variables affecting tourism at a particular destination along with dynamics of changes in motivation, preferences and expenditure pattern provide a clear idea about tourism demand. Multiplier effect on income and employment are negative where tourism demand decreases to a large extent over a particular period of time. Cross-border integration between firms of tourism sectors can bring significant welfare effects to countries and firms involved.

Malhotra, (1998) strongly favours straight – forward and cost effective methods while calculating tourism demand. Marketing strategies will be effective only when marketing plans are well understood and planned separately for each destination. When host community feelings are generally ignored while formulating methods for tourism promotion and development, drastic impact on destination are observed. Long-term and short-term strategies must be well utilised in achieving guest-host relationship for the very purpose of tourism to be successful.

Anson, (1999) while exploring the role of tourism in the aftermath of violence using the example of contested heritage of Northern Ireland finds, understanding the background of conflict is very important especially when tourism is considered as an integral part of post-conflict economic regeneration. Situations conducive for tourism business in affected region can be regenerated by facilitating interaction between people. Such interaction along with tourism business must be utilised for developing better political, socio-cultural and economic condition. While sharp downturn was observed in Northern Ireland's tourist inflow due to effects of terrorism, the 18 month cease-fire created new beginning for tourism enterprise as tourist inflow increased at the destination.

Sonmez, Apostolopoulos, & Tarlow, (1999) established that terrorism as tourism crises. Further random acts of terrorism curtail tourist liberty resulting in cancellation or avoiding risky destinations. Persistence of terrorism activities tarnish the destination image and completely ruin tourism industry. Media's improved ability in covering terror incidents increases the negative impact, especially among viewers. Terrorist choice of the tourist as target is not coincidental as they gain financially, tactically more and disturb tourism demand pattern by damaging positive image of the destination. While offering suggestions for managing the effects of terrorism on tourism, the authors recommend switching to recovery marketing techniques integrated with effective crises management techniques, increasing domestic tourist inflow, devising strategies to increase visitation, encouraging host community experts in image building exercise, working in close co-ordination with media, in-depth understanding between security officials and tourism stakeholders, practicing community policing and preparing to face future crises to avoid wastage of time and resources.

Evans, (2000) explains how Kashmir problem was dominated by guest militants with the help of Pakistan's Inter-Service Intelligence agency and how Indian counter measures and election in 1996 turned the situation in Kashmir. Though tourists ignored Kashmir for nine years from 1990, it is heartening to note the revival of tourist interest in Kashmir in 1999. Kargil intrusion dampened the spirit and tourists left the valley in May 1999. Knowledge of the organisation, structure, safety measures of security forces inspired terrorists to initiate attacks on bases of security forces. Failure on the part of State Government in bringing expected changes, IC 814 hijack in December 1999 and release of three hard core militants, failure in delivering normalisation through counter-terror policies, lack of political will and Pakistan's support increased terror activities and resulted in damaging the situation in Kashmir further.

Crenshaw, (2000) strongly advocates that in the absence of an universally accepted definition of terrorism, understanding terrorism through the result of psychopathology is not a logical method as terrorism is a group activity that too when groups feel threatened. A good number of research studies on terrorism and counter – terrorism policies being event-driven, a systematic analysis of motivation for renouncing terrorism which is essential for bringing the problem to an end is found missing. This being the main hurdle, the government follows forceful and punitive response mechanism to curb the terrorism in a short span of time. Such measures often backfire as they stimulate a desire for revenge and innovation of new strategies of terrorism. Counter-terrorism researches/policies can be effective and successful only when the models integrate individuals, groups and the society.

Albini (2001), examining the non conventional ways to be adopted by law enforcement agencies while dealing with modern terrorists using the Italian Red Brigades as a case study, finds the changed nature and composition of terrorism globally, which necessitates the exploration of methods for dealing with terrorists. Following old, backward or insensitive methods to overcome terrorism creates frustration, anger and inspires the terrorists to adopt modern tactics to take revenge. Terrorism reign came to an end in Italy when its citizens, government reached a consensus through thorough knowledge, understanding, and willingness that paved the way for reaching the minds and hearts of brigade members. As there is no particular method to deal with terrorism effectively, the State depends heavily on military and economic sanctions which are not effective against modern methods of terrorism. A fresh look at the root causes, actively engaging all interested citizens in surveillance against terror activities, and our willingness to adopt new non conventional approaches whenever possible will enable us to solve the problem of terrorism.

Frey & Lewchinger, (2002a) while designing superior strategies to deterrence, suggests that preventing potential terrorist from attacking and creating favourable consequences are the two important factors that cannot be ignored. Terrorist's main goals are; to destabilise the politics, damage the economy and seek publicity. Deterrence seeks to prevent terrorist act by making them more difficult to undertake. Extremist views are likely to flourish in isolated groups. Access to opportunities to visit other countries, monetary incentives, secured future, reduced punishment will induce terrorists to step out of terror organisations and reduces the inclination towards terrorism. Despite the strong deterrence strategies terrorist movements have survived, implying policy makers must utilise alternate mechanisms of deterrence and ways to reduce cohesiveness of the terror organisations. A mix of various strategies based on the type of terrorist orgsnisation, rather than the one exhibiting the robustness of the state, will fetch effective and favourable results.

Basrur, (2002) commenting on the process of change in Indian strategic thinking after Kargil conflict in 1999, insists for an alternative approach to tackle Pakistani intervention in Kashmir. After Kargil, a range of initiatives was subsequently undertaken to improve the political environment as a result of which the Agra summit took place. The depth of Pakistani involvement in Kashmir remained unchanged and India's conventional advantage was neutralised as they too had nuclear weapons. Later, India's idea of limited war with specific objectives convinced Pakistan that nuclear deterrence would not deter India from military action, and their support for terrorism in India will be a costly affair in future. Though India often speaks to strike against terrorist camps, such ideas are unlikely to destroy terrorism as the camps can simply shift their geographical location. Military solutions to the problem of terrorism are unlikely to fetch desired results, so there is a need for designing a non-military tool to fight terrorism. The author opines prolonged adherence to misunderstood notions of limited war and strategic space are not good sign for the region's future.

Gupta, Clements, Bhattacharya & Chakravarti, (2002) based on an empirical analysis of the fiscal effects of armed conflict and terrorism on low and middle income countries found reduced economic activity, negative growth, and changes in government spending as the main outcomes. Destruction of physical infrastructure and human capital has an indirect effect on trade, tourism, and business confidence which in turn adversely affect the economic growth. Conflict and terrorism affect the fiscal situation of the nation by influencing real economic activity (GDP) and government revenues, by affecting tax base and by changing the composition of government spending. Share of government revenue in GDP exhibiting the stage of development and the openness of the economy tends to fall during conflict period and pick up after post conflict period. Higher share of defence spending during conflict and terrorism divert resources away from socially and economically productive sectors and reduces growth of real per capita government spending on education and health. Countries that enjoy peace by tackling terrorism spend less on defence thereby funds can be used for other priority sectors. It also helps in restoring macroeconomic stability.

Habibullah, (2002) offered a first-hand account of the siege, at Hazratbal. He narrated the mishandling of the episode by New Delhi and the consequent collapse of civil administration. Shrine at Hazratbal houses a relic holy to all Kashmiri Muslims, the hair of the Prophet of Islam, the Moh-i-Muqaddas. Public tensions flared up and widespread demonstrations followed, when the Indian army's siege to flush out Kashmiri militants at the Hazratbal shrine started in October 1993. Securing public support for the Government's action in such a situation is the main reason for success as far as Hazratbal is concerned. Incidents at Fateh Kadal and at Bijbehara created changes in the mindset of the militants and they softened their stand exhibiting welfare of the local people. Public confidence increased when all militants surrendered. On the other hand, the siege at Charar-e- Sharief was conducted entirely by the security forces - the army, paramilitary, and police - with little civilian participation but in the end all attempts to save failed. Normally militants would never like to surrender and Governments also dislike providing safe passage as it will not solve the problem permanently. The author strongly favours dialogue alone as the solution to the problem rather than confrontation and every stakeholder must understand and believe in problem solving through dialogue.

Frey & Lewchinger, (2002b) studied demerits of deterrence. They find it is less effective than generally considered. Effective anti-terrorist policy must include decentralised decision-making, political power, market system and economic actors. Anti-terrorism policy makers believe deterrence increases the perceived cost of terrorism upwards and reduces the intensity and number of terror incidents. Terrorist always aim at achieving the attention of media, destabilise the politics, and damage the economy. Deterrence policy will be successful when targeted nation is large, productive and not fully employed. Decentralised activity, Political set up with different centers of decision-making, distribution of political powers between different political actors, and various levels of Government will help in solving the problem. Deterrence policy often increases political and economic centralization, in turn inducing the terrorists to attack. Deterrence mechanisms are widely adopted by Governments to exhibit determination to fight terrorism, but a more accommodative anti-terrorism policy is needed for better results.

Henderson, (2003) evaluated the implications of Bali bombing on tourism sector. Consequent to bombing, tourists, operators and investors avoided areas associated with danger. Tourism marketing and developing agencies played a crucial role in devising and implementing strategies to attract tourist back. Though visitors have been enticed to Blai from around the globe, the bombings instantly created aftershocks. There was a fall in tourist's arrivals due to travel advisories, reduced air transport services, and occupancy rates in large hotels. The bombing affected small enterprises, taxi drivers, the garment and souvenir sellers, tour guides, craftsmen, hawkers and vendors. In order to revive tourism, focus and priority was given to domestic tourism sector. Travel agents were advised to organize inexpensive tour packages and expert advices were solicited to rebuild the destination. Overseas marketing was deliberately put on a low key allowing time for memories to fade. Patriotic sentiment was used to increase inflow of domestic tourists'. Safety and security became central marketing themes. Adequate measures were widely publicised in both domestic and international media to regain traveler's confidence. Tourist destinations being potential targets for terrorists, recovery of tourism after such attacks widely depends upon Government's approaches in handling such complex situations.

Chen & Chen, (2003) attempted to assess terrorism effects on travel arrangements and tourism practices after September 11 WTC twin tower attack in USA. Airlines suffered decline in passenger load, followed by slump in hotel occupancy rate and heavy security deployment at highly rise buildings, heavily crowded public places, and in commercial complexes. Casinos, sporting events, state tourism, and international tourism received setback to maximum extent and US stock values went down by seven percent. People showed less interest in visiting New York and rather liked to visit beaches to avoid terror attacks. People feared to use air transportation.

When the fear of terror attack persists, new marketing ideas centered on community based tourism may reduce the impact of terror effect on travel business.

Blank, (2003) studied tactics and strategy used in Jammu and Kashmir, and found situation has improved than earlier. While Indian forces exerted pressure to prevent Pakistan from extending support to terrorists, Government tried to create international pressure on Pakistan's interference in Kashmir affairs. State Government has limited role to play as military, paramilitary and financial resources required for developmental activities are controlled by Central Government. Hurriyat interest in consulting with groups in Pakistan, and Pakistan's lack of interest to initiate change at Kashmir complicates the situation further. Objectionable long-term goals of Jihadist movement like liberation of Kashmir from Indian rule, expansion of Islamic Government finds no support from people of Jammu and Kashmir. Though Jihadists tried to expand their operational horizons beyond Kashmir by hijacking Indian airlines flight IC 814 from Kathmandu, attacking Parliament House at New Delhi, attacking Swaminarayan temple in Gujarat, they were not able to achieve their goal. Lack of strategic thinking, short-term tactical maneuvers, and work of Jihadist beyond the control of ISI handlers all made Kashmir problem more complicated.

Swami, (2003) while attempting to create a frame work to solve differences finds the contours of terrorism steadily increased from 1989 – 90. Laxity in proper vigil, efficient border management and counter infiltration measures enhanced the inflow of arms and ammunition towards India. Though Indian Security forces succeeded in controlling the situation against terrorism, it failed to provide safer life for people in Jammu and Kashmir as foreign terrorists have the ability to sustain terrorism. 'Healing Touch' policy worked in favour of the Government at the initial stage, but ended in regrouping and restructuring of terror operations as a result of which terrorist morale increased and intensified the attack on Security forces, thereby forcing to adopt tighter control over the terror organisation. Troop's build-up along LOC and India's demand for an end to cross- border terrorism has not deterred infiltrators from crossing the border as they received more support from Pakistan. Indian military establishment was unable to prepare a military, covert or economically workable response to put an end to this problem. Right from the beginning, till date a visible continuity of ideology thought and practice prevails among the whole spectrum of various terror groups in Jammu and Kashmir. Though a network prevails among all terror groups, clear cut distinctions also are found between various terror groups. It makes it difficult for policy makers to bring them together for reaching a common understanding. Failure of the Government in strongly defending its secular culture complicated the problem further. Solution to such an ongoing conflict is possible only when all involved understand others point of view and work towards achieving the desired goal.

Fair (2003) studied about India's experience in urban area military operations. He contends despite numerous operations by Indian forces in urban areas, India does not have conventional Military Operation on Urbanized Terrain (MOTU) doctrine. Indian security forces have a rich expertise in conducting urban operations. Peculiar nature of combat in built up areas hindered the ability of forces in achieving success easily. When unrelenting cordon-and-search operations helped in controlling the problem to a large extent, especially in Srinagar urban area in early 1990's, absence of multiple agencies and instutional mechanism in dealing with the operation at Charar e-Sharif resulted in communal unrest in the Valley in 1995. Though India managed urban operations efficiently due to its population management and psychological operations in counter insurgencies, threat of terror attacks in key wealth generating areas such as information technology, tourism destinations, and government offices can be dealt effectively only when the lessons learned from the past are utilised for successful operation in future.

Glaesser, (2004) clearly focused how crisis dampens the spirit of tourism industry. Though natural and manmade crisis affect tourism human triggered crisis are noticed and remembered for a long period of time. Early warning methods, detection of weak signals, utilising time and budget along with suitable marketing techniques are recommended, apart from strategic methods for averting crisis in tourism industry within a short period of time and in a cost effective manner.

Marks, (2004) attempted to assess insurgency or counter insurgency at macro, meso and micro level. At micro level, Moscow's defeat in intervention at Afghanistan encouraged Pakistan to support rival elements in Jammu & Kashmir to tread in the path of violence. Analysis at meso level established demography of Kashmir, its unemployed youths, inability of economy to absorb educated youth in employment are vital causes of terrorism activities. Micro level study at only one district Doda established that the situation is not normal though under control, due to presence of heavy security arrangements by the Government. Counter insurgency policies to *address root causes of terrorism and sustainable approaches to solve terrorism are yet to be formulated. The author widely acknowledged the Indian method of dealing with terrorism as a viable option especially when militants carry out suicidal attacks and receive constant support from across the border. Progress in such a situation is possible with the help of security forces, especially when moderate groups are willing to talk and other groups are determined to disturb any move towards peace by targeting innocent people.*

Rajagopalan, (2004) while investigating the reasons for the formation of Rashtriya Rifles found that the counter insurgency operations in North Eastern states, Punjab, Jammu and Kashmir, incapability of paramilitary forces in handling insurgencies increased immense pressure on army's conventional role. Falling within the ambit of army and Ministry of Defence for its operational and administrative purposes respectively, Rashtriya Rifles are the best equipped counter insurgency battalion in India. Permanent deployment at Jammu and Kashmir State gave an extra edge in intelligent operation though success rate of this battalion is not as high as that of army battalions. Rashtriya Rifles reduced the role of army battalions, but deployment of Warriors is still visible in counter Insurgency operations. Rashtriya Rifles has institutionalised rather than isolating Army's role in counter insurgency operation exhibiting more changes are required for developing appropriate tools for counter insurgency operations.

Frey, Luechinger & Stwtzer, (2004) in an empirical study established that it is impossible to come up with one single figure for economic damages caused by terrorism. The main strategy behind targeting tourism sector is to create economic damage for achieving their political goals. Impact of such attack varies considerably depending upon the structure of the tourism industry, terror organisation, and also differs over time. Terrorism gradually influences tourist's choice of destination and when occurs repeatedly will affect inflow towards neighbouring countries also. Apart from this, Foreign Direct Investment (FDI), savings, consumption pattern, transactional costs are also affected by terrorism. Stock market also crumbles down as security cost increases and expected profit level falls down considerably. Rise in transportation costs at major cities facing terror attacks regularly is not a new phenomenon. Expenses towards defence increases diverting the resources for welfare measure to security related expenses. People living in country facing terrorism regularly are less happy than people living in other regions not facing problem of terrorism.

Swami, (2004) outlined strategic circumstances leading to proxy war and effectiveness of Indian responses. Conscious of India's military might and in order to avoid conventional war, Pakistan increased the supply of arms and engaged India in proxy war especially at Jammu and Kashmir. Using porous border and local guides familiar with the passes across mountains on the Line of Control (LOC), Pakistan pushed arms and ammunition in huge quantities despite Indian troop's deployment in Jammu and Kashmir. Reduction in terror incidents, and military defeat in Kargil war hardly deterred Pakistan's interest in Jammu and Kashmir. Indian military build- up in 2002 turned the situation under control. Installation of physical barriers through fencing is not possible due to the peculiar terrain in Jammu and Kashmir. As such it will take a long time for sub-conventional war initiated by Pakistan to come to an ultimate end.

Sahay, (2004) while exploring the significance of the changing parameters of cross-border terrorism finds Kashmir Valley people will reject terrorism, if awareness regarding Pakistan's game plan is created. Geographical location of the state, lack of willingness in understanding political development in the rest of India, exploitation of Kashmiri people by Pakistan for its own advantage - all together created a worst situation in Kashmir Valley. Pakistan's unstinted support to terrorism in Kashmir Valley through well planned strategy in provoking religious sentiments. Apart from Pakistan's support to terrorism, failure of policies adopted by the Indian State complicated the situation to a large extent. ISI preaching's had gone deep into the minds of the people of Kashmir without understanding the real intention of Pakistan. People have to understand the strength of unity in diversity and strive hard to bring the problem to an end by supporting the process of democracy rather than adopting gun culture.

Mishra, (2005) examined the basic difference between India and Pakistan over Kashmir. He has split issue into four segments, namely, Pakistan's Kashmir policy, India's policy towards Kashmir, peace process and finally ways to solve the existing problem. Failure in securing the confidence of Kashmiri people frustrated Pakistan, but political developments in Kashmir gave an opportunity for Pakistan to interfere, initiate demographic changes through terrorism and paralysed normal life by creating and supporting several outfits to destabilise Jammu and Kashmir. Kargil intrusions, hijack of IC 814, attack on Jammu and Kashmir Assembly, attack on Indian Parliament, Kaluchak incident, to name the few, have deteriorated bilateral relations. Whenever, India viewed it as terrorism from across border Pakistan labels it as Kashmiris internal struggle. Numerous measures to offset impact of terrorism were initiated by India, apart from fencing to choke infiltration, strengthening of counter-terrorism grid, modernisation of Jammu and Kashmir police force, pinpointed counter-terrorist operations, improved border management, providing enhanced security cover. Initiatives like Elections, economic development, better employment opportunity, special financial packages, reduction in troops from South Kashmir have helped in winning the 'hearts and minds', reduced alienation, and increased morale of the people. While composite dialogue process, historic bus trip to Lahore and Lahore declaration eased the situation, unfortunately, Kargil intrusion, attack on Indian Parliament increased the rift between two nations. General Musharraf version of Kashmir solution attracted opposition even in Pakistan and failed to invoke much interest in India. Flexibility by all parties to arrive at a mutually agreed point is the need of the hour as different perspectives leave no scope for an acceptable solution.

Jafa, (2005) studied the operational strategy and tactics of police force in Jammu and Kashmir for defeating terrorism. Alienation of Kashmiri Muslims due to erosion of their cultural identity, suppression of political rights and unemployment among educated youth along with Pakistan's support form the root causes for terrorism activity in Jammu and Kashmir. Especially after the rigged election in 1987, majority of people hoped if militants could humble India they can achieve freedom also. Most of the local terror groups became defunct as police and army gained upper hand in 1992-93, creating the way for foreign terrorists to appear in Kashmir. Increased budget by ISI of Pakistan to sustain terrorism in Kashmir along with modern weapons created a dent in the peace and security of the region. Massive deployment of forces on ground is used as a viable strategy to control terrorism. Absence of people's support to security forces in curbing terrorism induced security forces to use excessive force in controlling the situation. Attitudinal change, better intelligence, less harassment to civilians during search operations, professional handling of unarmed protestors, increasing strike forces as per the threat level, introduction of women battalion, humanitarian services to the people by security forces, employment opportunity for youth in security forces according to the author provide a healing touch and will help in dealing terrorism firmly. Initiating proactive measures to help the masses will deter people's support to terrorism.

Salij, (2005) addressed the significance of ineffective methods of fighting terrorism. He defines terrorism as the unlawful application of violence or the threat of its application for political purposes and insists that the root cause of terrorism has to be sought out and then cured by means of moral persuasion. Complete eradication of terrorism from this world is a distant dream but, international community must strive hard to eliminate the sources and support base for terrorism. It is highly unfair to fight against terrorism without understanding, designing, and employing effective tested methods to control it. Such methods of fighting will be effective in controlling terrorism but, the suppressed people will rise against or will show their resistance one way or the other. Responsible thought and actions would avoid such loss but, it is unfortunate even today people consider it as a matter of pride to hold more weapons to establish their superiority over other nations. The author clearly supports the view that terrorism is a great evil to the peace of society and has to be eliminated with lesser evil approaches. Bartley, (2005) compares the art of terrorism and Sun Tzu's art of war, though there is no proof the terror leaders are following this literature. The author finds certain strategies that can be followed by modern military leaders while fighting against unconventional war of terrorism. Osama bin Laden has emerged a strong leader because from the beginning he lead a very strict life, stood with his fellowmen even in great dangers and set an example to all his followers as mentioned in Sun Tzu's art of war. Osama bin laden's vision, strategies and natural ability as an organizer attracted Muslims from various nations all over the globe under the single umbrella of international jihad. Planning was made and built up models were constructed to train the terrorists. Psychological training, use of technology and explosive handling, ultra modern destructive weapons training, and document tampering were imparted to the recruits as a result of which even today they were able to face challenge of superior armies. Effective human intelligence, secret methods in recruitment, fund collection all helped the terrorism to flourish. The author recommends that the leader of the army combating terrorism must understand the ground realities and follow the strategies as mentioned in Sun Tzu's art of war wherever applicable to emerge as a victorious leader.

Johnson, 2006 discussed the South Asian conflicts since 1947. He focused on the Kashmir dispute during 1947-2004. He believes the unique geographical position of Kashmir which provided a natural defence for British India, later became a bone of contention between India and Pakistan. Though, United Nation's intervention created the Line of Control (LOC),

Pakistan's shift towards American orbit and Indian tilt towards Soviet Russia paved the way for arms race in this region. War between the two nations in 1965, 1971, 1984 Saichen Glacier dispute, cross border support from Pakistan to separatists groups operating in Kashmir, altogether contributed the rise in insurgency against Indian army. Nuclear test in 1998 both by India and Pakistan, 1999 kargil conflict, terror attack on Indian parliament and movement of Indian army closer to border region created the worst situations between both countries. Interminable insurgency turned Kashmir a hell. Aggressive postures of both India and Pakistan to impress domestic audience added fuel to the existing fire. India's counterterrorism strategies and attempts to reintroduce normalcy through elections improved the situation to a large extent. The author strongly recommends scaling down the strength of armed forces in both sides to facilitate diplomatic and political settlement.

Tarlow, (2006) in this classical work of social theory of terrorism and tourism explained how in reality, terrorism cast its impact on world's most post modern industry - travel and tourism. Terrorism seeks to destroy modernity, creates a devastating impact on tourism industry as reputation of destinations once damaged will take a long time to recover. Hijacking of airplanes, terror attacks at major world events like Olympic Games, attacks at airports, plane bombings, attack on ground transport networks, attacks on hotels and restaurants are some of the main themes of terrorism casting negative impact on tourism industry. Publicity gained by the terror outfits after attacks, economic and inconsolable human loss, psychological hurt induced on the global viewers are the main reasons for targeting the tourism infrastructure and destinations. Travelers prefer to visit destinations that are safe and secure. Though highly trained and calculating professionals are acting behind the screen to destabilise economy and social order of the globe, still terrorism is viewed as the outcome of psychological, economic or political frustration.

Kydd &Walter, (2006) examined strategies of terrorism at global level. Terrorism was successful between1980 and 2003 mainly because of Governments policies towards dealing terrorism. Terrorists during this period used threats, attrition, intimidation, provocation, spoiling and outbidding strategies and derived desired results. Threats were used mainly to counter Government policies and to gain domestic population support for terrorism. Attrition inflicts high cost on enemy and intimidation is used for gaining greater control over population.

Provocation strategy is widely used to exhibit that Government forces are evil. Spoiling strategy is adopted when general relations or conditions seems to improve between various groups and Government. The author recommends framing counter – terrorism policies in such a manner which will not end in creating support for terrorism by the population is the best way for eradicating terrorism.

Kilcullen, (2006) argues counter – insurgency measures depends upon insurgency. Reluctance in accepting problem at earlier stages affects the counter insurgency effectiveness. Isolation of the enemy, reducing support to insurgents from people, marginalization of the enemy by denying the popular base are part of classical counter-insurgency policies. The classical counter-insurgency policies are found ineffective because terror organisation have close cooperation among them, communication through internet, support from local population enhances their morale. The author suggest success of counter – insurgency mainly depends upon willingness to admit error as it occur, and adopt tactical and strategic level changes as and when required while countering insurgency.

Mills, (2007) while discussing countering insurgencies, found understanding cultural sensitivity plays a vital role in solving it. Even addition of more troops, more political accommodation fails to fetch expected results as opponents react instantly to adjust and exploit the opportunities arising as conflict has become a way of life. Winning the heart and mind of the people by using soft power, switching from military based campaign to value-based political-cultural campaign, understanding cultural anthropology along with NGO's and the media are viewed as new thinking in solving the existing problem.

Gray, (2007) while explaining irregular warfare, contends that the state army will lose more strength and resources though they are more in numbers, superior in equipment, training facilities and discipline. Government's overreaction to terrorism activities often help in growth of terrorism. Difficulty in exactly locating the 'centre of gravity', inability to distinguish terrorists from civilian population make the situation further complicated. Patience, discipline, leadership quality, ability in correctly identifying terrorists, suitable policy to win hearts and minds of the local population, inducing irregular enemy to appear on open battle, fool proof protection to civilian population, quickly switching to new strategies in combating terrorism will minimize loss of man power and resources on the part of state forces in long run.

Miller, (2007) attempted to evaluate, the efficacy of harsh policies or providing treatment to root causes for eliminating terrorism is effective. He found both aggressive and soft responses encourage terrorism. The characteristic differences among different terrorist groups permit only certain counter-terrorism policies to be effective that too on a particular type of terrorism. Classification of the of state counter –terrorism policies into five different categories such as doing nothing, conciliation, legal reform, restriction, and violence finds that the state often employs combination of these policies to combat terrorism. Segregation and analysis of terrorist groups based on primary motivation as national, separatist, revolutionary, reactionary, and religious implies terrorism can't be defeated solely through the state intervention. Adoption of the focused case comparison method and using few critical cases along with scholarly assessments through establishing a combination of concessions, legal reforms and restrictions helps in dealing with national-separatist groups, and revolutionary groups. Democracies facing multiple terrorism due to numerous terror groups have to deal complex situation as no best policy is designed by counter-terrorism researchers globally.

Mahajan, (2007) in his work on multiculturalism in the age of terror narrates India encountered terrorism for more than a decade, has ridden out the challenges posed by terrorism without abandoning its commitment to multiculturalism mainly due to cultural and political context. Terror attacks in India never target any one particular community but, they instill fear among common people and increase the gap between different communities within the society. Counter-terrorism measures often fail to distinguish the terrorist and other members of that community. Terrorism forces people to take refuge indoors, strike multiculturalism, suppress people from opening debate and discussion thereby rising a severe threat to democracies. Despite frequent attacks of varying intensities in India, cultural difference has not emerged and multicultural strategies of accommodating diversity were not challenged. Muslims from India ignored terror networks and it has been a source of relief and pride for India revealing efficient democratic government and tolerance of the dominant culture. Tolerance of the dominant community, openness, willingness to accommodate all others, and deeper understanding contributes multiculturalism in India. Understanding of self, tolerance, harmony between communities, accepting the presence of different views, concern for feeling and sentiments for personal freedom, equality between members, and material well being - all will help in securing multiculturalism amidst terror activities in India.

Chenoweth & Lowham, (2007) in an attempt to explore alternative ways of understanding terrorist typologies stress the need of understanding the basic of terrorism tactics, destructiveness and target apart from motives, nationalities, and religions for better analysis and policy response. Cluster analysis is found as useful tool rather than measure of means, motives and opportunities which are used to discuss terrorist incidents traditionally. Moreover it also shows terrorism is not an isolated event emerging from a single religion or ideology, but a method of unconventional warfare used by different people and at different points of time to achieve political ends. Classification provides useful information on possible responses or prevention measures, risk assessments, and re-categorizations of attacks which are of immense importance for policy makers in the field of counter-terrorism.

Maheshwari, (2007) analysing operation Aman, initiative by CRPF to bridge the gap with people of J&K found numerous factors create mistrust in the minds of security force personnel and local population while tackling terrorism. Operation Aman was initiated in order to attain synergy in the approaches tackling terrorism. Alienation due to mistrust, easy exploitation of cultural indifferences, economic hardships because of topography and climate of the region, misunderstandings of motives, aims, modus operandi and procedures of the security forces are the key issues in tackling terrorism in J&K. To reach out to common people, media, especially television and radio was used extensively with regular broadcast of programmes such as Shagoofey, Hello Kashmir, Phone In, apart from broadcasting cultural programmes, musical jingles and documentary films on local themes. Adoption of villages, All India Study Tour Ehsas for children, promotion of sports and distribution of sports goods to various schools, organizing shows for local artists, medical camps for needy people, economic project for widows of militancy were carried out to increase the goodwill between defence forces and local people. Local culture and ethos were fully adopted and people were made to understand security forces are there to help people to stand firm on their foot, reclaim their rightful lives rather than depending on the forces. Interestingly, the number of attacks on security personnel reduced drastically after the launch of operation Aman in 2006. Thus, human interaction, when it is multi-dimensional is a two way process leads to lasting relationships.

Rajagopalan, (2007) dealt with India's counter – insurgency strategy. Author found India views terrorism as a political problem. India adopted soft approaches with minimum force utilisation and solve it. Globally armies adopt repressive measures and this forced terrorists to follow various guerrilla tactics which in turn compels state army to deploy more strength and undertakes large operations to hold territory. When state army maintain huge force to keep insurgents away from population and economic centers, terrorists used limited capacity to harass people by attacking at unexpected place and time. The author suggests modulate use of force along with political compromises will be more effective.

Muthanna, (2008) opined that fear and societal pressure are the major reasons among people for supporting terrorism. Forced migration, violence against democratic institutions, Pakistan's support for proxy war, domination of valley region in all aspects of Jammu and Kashmir affairs during 1989 – 2007 induced the counter terrorism forces to adopt searches, arrest, restriction on movements, adopting resources under the provisions of Armed Forces Special Power Act (AFSPA), people friendly military operations, operation Maitreyi, and operation Sadbhavana, assistance in natural calamities, organizing group tours etc, . Though stick and carrot method is widely adopted, the author foresees an effective and greater interaction with civil population will help in troop reduction and in bringing normal situation at the earliest. Jones, (2008) by approaching the Jammu and Kashmir conflict holistically, uncovers numerous reasons that pose a threat to the region. Sidelining reasonable 40 terrorist group Jammu Kashmir Liberation Front (JKLF), foreign terrorists with the help of Pakistan ISI flooded the Kashmir valley and disturbed the peace resulting in deployment of additional troops. Overstretched, poorly equipped soldiers and uncoordinated approaches benefited terrorist. Despite various stringent measures to curb terrorism, terrorist tactics of using civilians as shield while attacking on security forces incurred more loss to security force, and paved the way for more troop deployment. Adopting conventional warfare strategies, lack of vital intelligence input along with unpopular search operations spoiled civilian-military relations. Violence continued even after the elections of 1996. Responsible reply to Kargil intrusion, tight security arrangements at Kashmir valley made terrorists to shift the focus and attack the targets away from Kashmir valley. Designing and implementing non-military tools to fight terrorism and fundamental societal changes in Pakistan will put an end to the prevailing Kashmir problem.

Nance, (2008) introduced a thorough explanation of how terrorist frame their strategies and select the target. Terrorists often use simple strategies, but often people misinterpret make *the situations complex. Terrorists plan well before any attack and attacks are never random, as speed, surprise and violence exhibited during such attacks creates maximum negative impact. On identifying the target as hard or soft, terrorists on the basis of motives, opportunity, and means carry out attack. Terrorists intensify the attack irrespective of target categories in order to degrade ability and the image of state security forces. Experts have to understand the strategies of terror organisations in order to predict terrorist's future course of action and plan meticulously to take the initiative away from them.*

Aran & Leon (2008) adopt a discrete choice approach to the study of the impact of terrorism on tourism demand and tourist preferences for alternative destinations and product attributes. The authors choose two competing destinations in the Mediterranean and the Canary Islands, by comparing the results of the two studies conducted with the same methodology just before and after the September 11 attacks in New York City. The study indicated that the impact of the 2001 incident on tourist preferences remained the same regardless of the socioeconomic characteristics of both the groups. The evaluation of the monetary impact shows a considerable decline in mean consumer surplus after the terror attacks. Major terrorist attacks and the corresponding impact are likely to affect both the decision to travel and individual's preferences towards attributes of the tourism product. As tourists' are particularly relevant for the image value of the destinations, authorities should anticipate and prevent major terror attacks, and their consequences.

Toshkhani, (2008) while estimating the nature and extent of the cultural loss suffered by the displaced Kashmiri Pundits found terrorists brutally devastated the valley - 'clone of paradise'. Kashmiri Hindus bore brutalities, forcible conversions and wanton destruction by resilience and self-preservation. Fundamentalists forced Kashmiri Hindus to migrate to prove a point that non-Muslims have no place in Kashmir. Displaced Kashmir's, especially younger generations faced numerous cultural problems. Having less chance to meet their own people except in occasions like marriages, sacred thread investiture and funeral rites their cultures are influenced by the place where they stay at present. Terrorism has reduced them as refugees in their own land and the author strongly favours minority status for such displaced people.

Goswami, (2009) analysed the merits and demerits of 'trust and nurture' strategy in counter –insurgency operations. He found that distrust existing between security forces and local population is the main hurdle in solving the problem. Fear, self-preservation and feeling of relative deprivation prevail in the insurgency affected population especially at remote in accessible terrains. Understanding by security forces regarding local customs, social behaviour, habits and ideologies will help in solving the problem. Strategy of 'trust and nature' can be developed through democratic political culture, well measured military methods, special counter insurgency forces, local social and cultural awareness. Though change in approaches is hard to digest by army researches in similar subjects will help to solve the problem effectively. Ismail,

Suhartono, Yahaya & Efendi, (2009) presented theoretical and empirical evidences in their study on the intervention model. The empirical study focused on Bali illustrated and explained the quantity and the time span of the first Bali bomb effect on the occupancy level of five star hotels in Bali and observed a decreasing trend for over a period of time in tourist arrival in Bali, Indonesia. Effects of terrorism on tourism industry are classified into three types such as temporary, gradual and permanent which are further estimated with the help of the model. A new model building procedure with three main steps for determining an intervention model was proposed for further research related to time series model that contains regime change, caused by intervention of pulse function and/or step function.

Piazza, (2009) examined the factors that contribute to terrorism. In the opinion of the author, finds poor economic development is not the only reason but unresolved and poorly managed political conflicts are chiefly responsible reason for terrorism in India. As Jammu and Kashmir State alone witnessed more terror activities than any other State in India, State wise terror incidents along with casualty rates from 1998 to 2006 are taken and a State Development Index (SDI) for each state is drawn. It was found that no statistically significant relationship exists between terrorist incidents or terrorist casualties and the raw SDI score of states. Six sources of political conflict, namely separatist movements, ethnic conflict, communal conflict, the presence of scheduled castes and tribes, high population growth, and the phenomenon of stateless areas are disproportionately present in the more terrorism prone states of India adding more complexity to problem solving. India's counter terrorism policies are ineffective especially in a state like Jammu and Kashmir as they failed to win the hearts and minds of the common people.

The review of literature reveals that Tourism the Backbone of Jammu and Kashmir economy slowly lost its prominence as increase in terror activities decreased the tourist inflow towards Kashmir valley. Centre of Gravity in case of terrorism in Jammu and Kashmir is from across the border and requires long-term strategy to tackle effectively as planning and support originate from Pakistan. Repeated outbreak of terror incidents with varying intensity created a feeling of alienation and crippled tourism activities. Increased security attracted tourist inflow but Kargil intrusion and situation aftermath forced to maintain heightened and vigilant security round the clock and year around making demilitarization or reduction in the strength of security forces at Jammu and Kashmir a distant dream. Knowledge of the non-military tools in eradicating terrorism still remains an unexplored area as a result globally policy makers tend to use force to solve the problem of terrorism. The use of non-military tools to eradicate terrorism, and strategies to win the hearts and minds of common people, has to be adopted to bring the situation back to normal. Therefore, the present study discuss the impact of terrorism on Kashmir valley domestic tourism, presence of security force and its effect on domestic tourist inflow and exploring strategies and techniques in adopting tourism as non-military tool to eradicate terrorism in the long run from the state. This present work is a continuum of existing literature especially to remove the roadblocks to tourism development created by terrorism activities.

IMPACT OF TERRORISM ON TOURISM IN JAMMU & KASHMIR

"Don't let the evil actions of broken people define your view of our world! Don't be terrorized into a diluted, hopeless reality"

(Dr.Steve Maraboli)

Annals of history prove terrorism solves no problem in the world. Not understanding this fully, certain emotionally charged individuals persist in the use of terrorism to achieve their goals. Though they have not achieved the goals, it becomes the duty of the researchers to look into the issue and expose the reality so that future generations will learn the lessons that terrorism serves no purpose except destructions. Understanding terrorism itself is a complex phenomenon. It is necessary to understand the processes that have made terror a mutant of war by itself (Singh, 2000). This is quite true of this study as well, since terrorism in Jammu and Kashmir is the results of various incidents that took place before and after independence of India. Most thinkers, historically, are in favor of violence as a response to conflict, or at least some conflict (Hastings, 2004) as a result of which violence continues to grow without any hindrance. Terrorism being a complex problem extends over a long Complexity Time Scale Epistemology period and requires a thorough knowledge of its root causes. Kashmir Valley, of Jammu and Kashmir State, known for its natural beauty and cultural heritage, surrounded by mountains carpeted by snow is pertinently referred to as "The Paradise on Earth". "From an English point of view the valley contains nearly everything which should make life enjoyable. There is sport varied and excellent, there is scenery for the artist and layman, mountains for the mountaineer, flowers for the botanist, a vast field for the geologist and magnificent ruins for the archaeologist"- The Valley of Kashmir (1895) -Travel Book by Sir Walter Roper Lawrence. The land of such strategic location with rare concoction of mountains, lakes, forests, fertile land, tulip gardens, splendid blue skies and rich cultural heritage used to be flocked by tourists from times immemorial till peace of this land of unending glory was disrupted by the terror groups in early 1990's, which led to loss of tourism revenue, creating an economic vacuum in the Valley. The three decades long armed conflict and geo-political instability has impacted every socioeconomic activity in Kashmir Valley. Besides art and crafts sectors, tourism has been the worst hit of this continuous unrest. Peace, conflict and revenue generating sectors like tourism, arts and crafts and apple orchards (in case of the Valley) anywhere in the world are intertwined and disturbances in any of the three impacts the other two. Regardless of the abundance of scenic beauty and rich cultural heritage, the constant fear of death and continued unrest led to the loss of tourist appetite for this destination. As per the available data, the tourist arrival was prodigious 0.72 million in 1988, followed by a drastic dip in 1991, when it was reduced to mere 6287 tourists annually. Ordinarily, a traveler has two questions: "where" and "how" to travel but when it comes to Jammu and Kashmir, the question changes to "whether" to travel or not. "Unless terrorism is viewed as a crisis by the tourism industry, energy and resources cannot be effectively channeled into its management"- Sevil.F Sonmez (1999)- Speaker-University of Central Florida, occupational/leisure/health. Historical sites and other tourist spots have either been in use by the military or have become hideouts and safe havens for terrorists. The security experts state that they have no other option than to use large number of troops to mitigate challenges thrown by terrorism. From the point of view of tourism, whether or not there should be Army troops in large numbers is debatable, as the native population feels presence of security forces and infrastructure raised by them is the primary hindrance for tourist inflow, whereas tourists traveling to Kashmir valley feel presence of security forces psychologically motivates them to visit Kashmir and makes them feel safer. The year 1987, pre-terrorism period was the last big revenue generating season for Jammu and Kashmir tourism, and accounted for approximately 10% of the State's income, while the following 29 years contributed virtually nothing. The international tourists constituted a significant percentage of the tourists visiting Kashmir, who spent large sums on handicraft products, and invested in adventure sports like trekking, skiing and rafting. However, there have been series of headline grabbing incidences, especially the one in 1995 when some foreign tourist trekkers were kidnapped by terrorists, among whom one was be-headed, one escaped and other four untraced, who were later declared as dead, which proved to be a major blow for FTAs (Foreign Tourist Arrivals). As a consequence of this specific incident negative travel advisories to visit Kashmir were issued by foreign nations, adversely affecting the tourist revenue generated by foreign visitors. Attacking international tourists works in favor of terror groups, as it leads to higher media- and international attention and spreads terror among the local community. Besides foreign nationals, Indian tourists were also targeted. The Srinagar International Airport witnessed three major terror attacks and Srinagar was once declared as the most threatened site in India by the World Monuments Fund (WMF), placing it on the 2008 List of Most Endangered Sites. It is estimated that the State of Jammu and Kashmir lost around 27 million tourists from 1989-2002, leading to a tourism revenue loss of 3.6 billion USD and consequent high unemployment. The owners of hotels, guest houses and houseboats, whose business is completely dependent upon the inflow of tourists suffered major economic losses. Nearly 1094 houseboats in Dal Lake, Nigeen Lake and River Jhelum and all those people employed in their running were rendered idle, forcing them to look for alternative sources of income. The employability in this sector will continue to be volatile as any terror attack would mean loss of business for tourism industry and impact handicraft, carpet industry, hotel industry which are majorly dependent on tourism. The handicraft industry, providing employment to more than 300,000 people, has witnessed a drastic dip in the production of art work like paper mache items, wooden art-ware and Kashmiri rugs, which are highly appreciated and purchased by (international) tourists. Impact of Hartals (Shutdowns) and curfews In today's age of Internet of Things (IoT) instead of using modern means of communication to put forth their demands and reach out to larger masses, the separatists groups opt to rely upon Hartals (strikes) and shutdowns, thereby making people abstain from work. The unending era of strikes is as old as terrorism in the Kashmir Valley, where from an arrest of a militant commander to the killing of a civilian, is followed by week long strikes which gradually decayed the economy of the State. There have also been times when strikes were enforced by separatist and terrorists upon the people of Kashmir because of unrelated incidents happening in the larger Muslim world. These strikes have failed to attract international attention and lost their relevance nationally, as they remain localized to few localities of Srinagar and other towns in the State. The daily wagers, street vendors, passenger bus drivers, conductors, fruit sellers, who must step out of the house every day to be able to feed themselves and people dependent on them, are the primary and worst casualties of the shutdowns and continue to suffer silently. The curfew which was imposed on 18th July 2016, which started after the unrest in response to the killing of Burhan Wani, was one of the harshest ever curfews which continued for a period of six months across all ten districts of Kashmir. For the initial 51 days of the curfew, people remained confined to the four walls of their houses without a break or what is referred to in Kashmir as "deal". Curfew remained in place strictly during days as well as nights. The Jammu based business claimed to have suffered an estimated loss of 1.5 billion USD in those 51 days of Hartal and curfew as Kashmir receives majority of supplies from edibles to industrial goods from Jammu where major industries of the State are situated. Most of the multinational companies supplying edibles to the State have stationed their forwarding agents in Jammu, therefore all the supplies that are meant to reach Kashmir are bound to pass through the Jammu region. The tourist arrival went down from 12,000 tourists to 250 per day with hotel and houseboat occupancy around 3%; The Valley was reduced to just being a stopover destination for tourists visiting Ladakh. Kashmir is one of the largest producers of apples; 70% of apples that are sold in mainland India are from Kashmir. For fruit growers/farmers/vendors, these Hartals meant that daily produce of fruit could not be transported to outside markets and since there is not a single cold storage in Srinagar, the fruits if not sold or transported to outside markets, got rotten effecting the business on a daily basis. It is estimated that due to persistent shutdowns, fruit growers have incurred a loss of 1.24 to 1.4 billion USD. Horticulture is the mainstay of Kashmir's economy, with 2300,000 people associated with this sector. More than 1301.16 sq. miles are under fruit cultivation in Jammu and Kashmir, of which 841.70 sq. miles of land is under the fruit cultivation in the Valley, of which 65 per cent comprises of apple orchards. Going by conservative estimates, from horticulture to hospitality, a loss of over 9.33 million USD has been incurred during the 51 days long Hartals and curfews. Others affected by Hartals, are people associated with art and craft industry, who find neither transporters nor any buyers for their shawls and artwork. The strikes have had adverse effects on other aspects of life like education and healthcare. The educational institutions remain shut during hartals with children losing days and sometimes months of their academic calendar and the sick unable to access medical help. It is hard to comprehend why the "Hartal strategy" is never debated by separatist groups or the population as to why it is the preferred strategy to make their presence felt in the valley. These unnecessary calls for shutdowns have outlived their utility; the only achievement so far has been putting the lives of common man in danger and making survival difficult.

"The study of psychological motivations for terrorism, as well as for ending terrorism, should continue to be based on a model that integrates the individual, the group, and society" (Crenshaw, 2000) The issue of terrorism needs to be addressed through both long – term and short - term approaches. It calls for a multi-pronged approach. It requires efforts by tourism authorities both at state and central level, tourist marketers, wholesalers, and independent travel agents both within the Kashmir Valley and at other tourism generating markets throughout India. People must remember that in the fight against terrorism we must not allow the peace loving individuals to suffer. A prolonged usage of military strategies has an adverse impact on people as well as on security force also. A suitable mix of military and non-military strategies is *the need of the hour. When all the people of India stand together along with security forces, express whole hearted concern for Jammu and Kashmir brothers and sisters, and show the support to them in the fight against terrorism by visiting them once in our lifetime, it will certainly tone down terrorism. As such, tourism is the major non-military approach as it has the power to bring people together, and initiate change in the minds of misguided people who adopted terrorism as their strategy to achieve the ill founded goals.*

REFRENCES

Albini, J. L., (2001). *"Dealing With the Modern Terrorist: The Need for Changes in Strategies and Tactics in the New War on Terrorism", Criminal Justice Policy Review, Vol.12, No. 4, December, pp. 255-281.*

Anson, C., (1999). *"Planning for peace: The role of Tourism in the Aftermath of Violence", Journal of Travel Research, Vol. 38, No. 57, August, pp. 57-61. Aran, J. E., & Leon, C J., (2008). "The Impact of Terrorism on Tourism Demand", Annals of Tourism Research, Vol. 35, No. 2, pp. 299 -315.*

Bartley, C. M., (2005). *"The Art of Terrorism: What Sun Tzu can Teach us about International Terrorism", Comparative Strategy, 24:3, pp. 237- 251. Basrur, R. M., (2002). "Kargil, Terrorism, and India's Strategic Shift", India Review, vol. 1, No. 4, October, pp. 39-56.*

Bammi, Y.M., (2007). *War against Insurgency and Terrorism in Kashmir, Nataraj Publishers, Dehradun, pp. 147-48.*

Beanlands, G.E., & Duinker, P.N., (1983). *An Ecological Framework for Environmental Impact Assessment in Canada. Institute for Resource and Environmental studies, Dalhousie University, Halifax. Betz, D., (2007). "Redesigning Land Forces for Wars Amongst the People" Contemporary Security Policy, Vol. 28, No. 2, August, pp. 221-243.*

Blank, J., (2003). *"Kashmir: All Tactics, No Strategy". India Review , Vol.2, No.3, pp. 181-202. Chen, R. J. C., & Chen, J. S., (2003). "Terrorism Effects on Travel Arrangements and Tourism Practices", International Journal of Hospitality & Tourism administration, Vol.4, (3), pp. 49-63.*

Bowman, B. L., (2007). *"US Grand Strategy for Countering Islamist Terrorism and Insurgency in the 21st Century", In James.J.F.Forest, (Eds.), Countering Terrorism and Insurgency in the 21st Century International Perspectives, Vol. 1, Praeger Security International, London, pp.29-55.*

Bukhari, S., (2010). *(as quoted by Mirwaiz Umar Farooq), "Amarnath Yatra beigns on Smooth note with 15,000 Yatris", The Hindu, 02 July, p. 13.*

Chellaney, B., (2008). "Defensive measures alone won't suffice", The Hindu, 20 December, Chennai, p. 10.

Chenoweth, E., & Lowham, E., (2007). "On Classifying Terrorism: A Potential Contribution of Cluster Analysis for Academics and Policy-makers", Defense & Security Analysis Vol. 23, No. 4, December, pp. 345-357.

Crenshaw, M., (2000). "The Psychology of Terrorism: An Agenda for the 21 st Century", Political Psychology, Vol. 21, No. 2, pp. 405- 420.

Doval, A., (2007). "Needed War on Error", The Indian Express, 30 August, Pune. Glaesser, D., (2004). (as quoted by Krampe and Muller, 1981). "Crisis Management in the Tourism Management Industry", Elsevier Butterworth-Heinemann, Oxford pp. 142-143.

Evans, A., (2000). "The Kashmir Insurgency: As bad as it gets", Small Wars & Insurgencies, Vol. 11, No.1, pp. 69-81.

Fair, C. C., (2003). "Military Operations in Urban Areas: The Indian Experience", India Review, Vol. 3, No. 1, January, pp. 49-76.

Frey, B. S., & Luechinger, S., (2002a). "How to Fight Terrorism, Alternatives to Deterrence", Working Paper Series ISSN 1424-0459, Working, Paper No.137, Institute for Empirical Research in Economics, University of Zurich, December.

Frey, B. S., & Luechinger, S., (2002b). "Terrorism: Deterrence May Backfire", Working Paper Series ISSN 1424-0459, Working Paper No. 136, Institute for Empirical Research in Economics, University of Zurich, December.

Frey, B. S., Luechinger, S., & Stwtzer, A., (2004). "Calculating Tragedy: Assessing the Cost of Terrorism", Working Paper No.205, Institute for Empirical Research in Economics, University of Zurich, and September.

Friedland, N., & Merari, A., (1985). "The Psychological Impact of Terrorism: A Double-Edged Sword", Political Psychology, Vol. 6, No. 4, December, pp. 591- 604.

Glaesser, D., (2004). *Crisis Management in the Tourism Industry*, Elsevier Butterworth-Heinemann, London.

Goswami. N., (2009). "India's Counter - Insurgency Experience: The Trust and Nature Strategy", *Small Wars & Insurgencies*, Vol. 20, No.1, March, pp. 6981.

Gray, C. S., (2000). *War, Peace and International Relations An Introduction to Strategic History*, Routledge, Oxon, pp. 245- 263.

Gupta, S., Clements, B., Bhattacharya, R., & Chakravarti, S., (2002). "Fiscal Consequences of Armed Conflict and Terrorism in Low - and Middle-Income Countries", *IMF Working Paper No.WP/02/142*, Fiscal Affair Department.

Gray, C. S., (2007b). "Irregular Warfare Guerrillas, Insurgents and Terrorists", *War Peace and International Relations An Introduction to Strategic History*, Routledge, London, pp. 245-248.

Gurung, S., (2006). "A Viable Strategy to Fight Proxy War in J & K", *NDC.Paper 2006*, p. 1, http://ndc.viburnix.com/pages/research-thesis? accessed on 29 June 2010.

Habibullah, W., (2002). "Siege: Hazratbal, Kashmir, 1993", *India Review*, Vol. 1, No. 3, July, pp. 73-98. Henderson, J. C., (2003). "Terrorism and Tourism: Managing the Consequences of the Bali Bombings", *Journal of Travel & Tourism Marketing*, Vol.15, (1), pp. 41-58.

Hameel, Y., (2010). (as quoted by Salahuddin supreme commander of Hazibul Mujahideen in a telephonic interview), "130 Bilateral Talks but No Solutions" *Deccan Chronicle*, 14 Feb, Chennai, p. 11.

Hewitt, V., (2003). "An Area of Darkness, Still? The political Evolution of Ethnic Identities in Jammu and Kashmir, 1947-2001", In Rajat Ganguly and Ian Macduff , (Eds.), *Ethnic Conflict and Secessionism in South and South East Asia Causes, Dynamics, Solutions*, Sage, New Delhi, pp. 59- 98.

Ismail, Z., Suhartono, Yahaya, A., & Efendi, R., (2009). "Intervention Model for Analyzing the Impact of Terrorism to Tourism Industry", Journal of Mathematics and Statistics, Vol. 5, (4), pp. 322-329.

Jafa, Y. S., (2005). "Defeating Terrorism: A Study of Operational Strategy and Tactics of Police Forces in Jammu & Kashmir (India)", Police Practice and Research, Vol. 6, No. 2, May, pp. 141–164.

Johnson, R., (2006). "The Kashmir Dispute, 1947-2004", in A Region in Turmoil South Asian Conflicts since 1947, Viva Books Pvt Ltd, New Delhi, pp. 91-116.

Jones, S., (2008). "India, Pakistan, and counter Insurgency Operations in Jammu and Kashmir", Small Wars & Insurgencies, Vol. 19, No.1, March, pp. 1-22.

Kilcullen, D., (2006). "Counter-Insurgency Redux", Survival, The IISS Quarterly, Vol.48, No.4 , (Winter), pp. 111-130.

Kishore, S., (1987). National Integration in India, Sterling Publishers Pvt Ltd, New Delhi.

Kydd, A. H., & Walter, B. F., (2006). "The Strategies of Terrorism", International Security, Vol. 31, No. 1 , (Summer), pp. 49-80.

Mahajan, G., (2007). "Multiculturalism in the Age of Terror: Confronting the Challenges", Political Studies Review, Vol. 5, pp. 317-336.

Maheshwari, A. P., (2007). "Operation Aman a CRPF Initiative on Bridging Gap with People of J & K", The Indian Police Journal, Vol. LIV No. 4, October-December. pp. 20-26.

Malhotra, R. K., (1998). Tourism Marketing, Anmol Publication Pvt Ltd, New Delhi.

Marks, T. A., (2004). "India State Response to Insurgency in Jammu Kashmir–The Jammu Case", Low Intensity Conflicts & Law Enforcement, Vol.12, No.3,

Autumn, pp.122-143. Miller, G. D., (2007). "Confronting Terrorisms: Group Motivation and Successful State Policies", Terrorism and Political Violence, 19:3, pp. 331– 350.

Mills, G., (2007). "New Thinking on Countering Insurgencies", Pakistan Horizon, Vol. 60, No.3, July, pp.99-107.

Misra, A., (2005), "The Problem of Kashmir and the Problem in Kashmir: Divergence Demands Convergence", Strategic Analysis, Vol. 29, No.1, JanMar, pp.16-42.

Muthanna.K. A., (2008). "Counter Terrorism Operations in Kashmir Valley Contest For Hearts and Minds of the People", Journal of the United Service Institution of India, Vol.CXXXVIII, No.572, April – June, pp. 213-224.

Nance, M. W., (2008). "Terrorist Strategies and Target Selection" in Terrorist Recognition Handbook, Second Edition, CRC Press, Boca Raton, pp. 91 -101.

Piazza, J. A., (2009). "Economic Development, Poorly Managed Political Conflict and Terrorism in India", Studies in Conflict & Terrorism, Vol. 32 No. 5, September-October, pp. 406 - 419.

Pope, A. In H. Rawson & M. Miner, (1986). "The New International Dictionary of Quotations", E. P. Dutton, New York, p. 70.

Rajagopalan, R., (2004). "Innovations in Counter Insurgency the Indian Army's Rashtriya Rifles", Contemporary South Asia, 13, (1), March, pp. 25- 37.

Rajagopalan, R., (2007). "Forces and Compromise: India's Counter- Insurgency Grand Strategy", South Asia: Journal of South Asian Studies, Vol.XXX, No.1, April, pp. 75-91. Sahay, A. K., (2004). "Changing Parameters of Cross-Border Terrorism in Kashmir", International Studies 41, 2, pp.185-194.

Salij, J., (2005). "The Significance of Ineffective Methods of Fighting Terrorism", American Behavioral Scientist, Vol. 48, No. 6, February, pp. 700-709.

Sinclair, M. T. & Stabler, M., (1997). The Economics of Tourism, Routledge, London. Singh, S., (1986). A Strategy for Indian Defence, Lancer International, New Delhi.

Sonmez, S. F., Apostolopoulos, Y., & Tarlow, P., (1999). "Tourism in Crisis: Managing the Effects of Terrorism", Journal of Travel Research, Vol. 38, August, pp.13-18.

Swami, P., (2003). "Terrorism in Jammu and Kashmir in Theory and practice", India Review, vol. 2, No. 3, pp. 55- 88. Swami, P., (2004). "Failed Threats and Flawed Fences: India's Military Responses to Pakistan's Proxy War", India Review, vol. 3, No. 2, April, pp. 147-170.

Tarlow, P. E., (2006). "A Social Theory of Terrorism and Tourism", In Yoel Mansfield and Abraham Pizam, , (Eds.), Tourism Security and Safety from Theory to Practice, Elsevier, Amsterdam, pp. 33 – 48.

Toshkhani, S. S., (2008). "Terrorism in Jammu & Kashmir – the Cultural Dimension", Dialogue, Vol.9, No. 4, April-June, pp. 83-96. Uberoy, U., (1989). "Approach to Anti-Terrorism" In Combating Terrorism, Directory Publication, Ambala, pp. 98-123.

Gray, C. S., (2007a). "Irregular Warfare Guerrillas, Insurgents and Terrorists", War Peace and International Relations An Introduction to Strategic History, Routledge, London, p. 247.

Jagmohan, (2008). "Counter Terrorism Lessons from J & K", Deccan Chronicle, 15 December, Chennai, p. 10.

Karnad, B., (2001). "A New Strategy for the LOC and Low-intensity warfare in Kashmir", In K. P. S. Gill, (Eds.), Terror and Containment Perspectives of India's Internal Security, Gyan Publishing House, New Delhi, pp.141-159.

Kumaraswamy, S., (2008). (as quoted by Lt.Gen. Kadyan), "When Olive Green Turns Red", Deccan Chronicle Sunday Special, 16 November, Chennai, p. 10.

Latham, J., & Edwards, C., (2006). "The Statistical Measurement of Tourism", In Chris Cooper, (Eds.), Classical Reviews in Tourism, Viva Books, New Delhi, pp. 55-76.

Mack, A., (1987). "Why Big Nation Lose Small Wars: The Politics of Asymmetric Conflict", In Kluas Knorr , (Eds.), A World Politics Reader Power, Strategy, and Security, Asian Book, New Delhi, pp. 127-151.

Radhakrishnan, R. K., (as quoted by General Deepak Kapoor, Chief of Army Staff), (2009). "Troops Well Deployed to Check Infiltration", The Hindu, 20 September, Chennai, p. 9.

Rane, P.P., (2007). "Counter-Terrorism Strategies: India's Option", In Gautam Sen , (Eds.), *Impediments to National Security*, National Centre of International Security and Defence Analysis, p. 376.

Richardson Jr, J. M., (2003). "Costs of Terrorism ., & Deadly Conflicts Who Should Care & Why Should They Care", In Sridhar K Khatri and Gret W. Kueck, (Eds.), *Terrorism in South Asia Impact on Development and Democratic Process*, Shirpa Publication, New Delhi. p. 33.

Ritchie, J.R.B., (1975). "Some Critical Aspects of Measurement Theory and Practice in Travel Research", In R.W. Mc. Intosh and C.R. Goeedner, (1986) *Tourism Principles, Practices, Philosophies*, John Wiley, New York, pp. 437-451.

Seymour, M., & Moore, S., (2000). "Effective Crisis Management Worldwide Principles and Practice", Cassel, London, p. XVII. (Introduction).

Singh, A. & Singh, R., (2009). (as quoted by Vajpayee, Former Prime Minister of India), "Prevention and Preparedness To Counter Terrorism For Sustainable Growth of Tourism", *Indian Journal of Applied Hospitality & Tourism Research*, Vol. 1, January, p. 9.

Sonmez, S., Apostolopoulos, Y., & Tarlow, P., (1999). "Tourism in Crisis: Managing the Effects of Terrorism", *Journal of Travel Research*, Vol. 38, August, pp. 1318.

Thampu, V., (2008). "Give ahimsa a chance", *The Hindu*, 09 November, Chennai, p. 5

The Hindu, (2010). "Kashmir's Street War", Editorial, *The Hindu*, 02 July, Chennai, P. 10.

Treweek, J., (1999). *Ecological Impact Assessment*, Blackwell Science, Oxford, p. 155.

Uberoy, U., (1989). "Approach to Anti-Terrorism", in *Combating Terrorism*, Directory Publication, Ambala Cant.p.107.

White, J. R., (2002). *Terrorism An Introduction*, Thomson Wadsworth, Canada, p. 16.

Wilkinson, P., (1986a). "Terrorism", In Lunis Pauling , (Eds.), *World Encyclopedia of Peace*, Vol.2, Pergamon Press, Oxford, p. 452.

Wilkinson, P., (1986b). "Terrorism", In Lunis Pauling, (Eds.), World Encyclopedia of Peace, Vol.2, Pergamon Press, Oxford, p. 457.